TRANSPARENT

TRANSPARENT

CNN ANCHOR AND SPECIAL CORRESPONDENT

Don Lemon

Farrah Gray Publishing

www.fgpbooks.com

ISBN-13: 978-0-9827-0278-9
ISBN-10: 0-9827-0278-7
ISBN-13: 978-0-9727-0993-4 (e-books)
ISBN-10: 0-9727-0993-2 (e-books)

Farrah Gray Publishing, its logos, and its marks are trademarks of Farrah Gray Publishing

Publisher: Farrah Gray Publishing
     P.O. Box 33355
     Las Vegas, NV 89133

Karyn Langhorne Folan
Dr. Marcia Brevard Wynn
Cover Photo John Nowak ©2011 Cable News Network. A Time Warner Company. All Rights Reserved.

CONTENTS

Part One: Family and Foundation

Part Two: You Don't Want to Fail on a Stage That Big

Part Three: Chicago

Part Four: My Life at CNN

Conclusion: Full Circle

FOREWORD

I was a kid who felt "different" from other kids.

I was a kid who lived in fear of other kids.

I was a kid who was bullied by other kids.

I know what it feels like to think that one is completely alone.

Thankfully, I survived those moments. I lived through them and past them, into better moments. I lived through them and past them, into moments that taught me that even when I felt most alone, I wasn't.

As I grew older and became more successful in my career, those dark moments faded deep into my memory. They were almost a thing of the past, until I heard the story of Tyler Clementi.

Tyler Clementi was a gifted violinist and student at Rutgers University who had a promising future. Sadly, he never got the chance to enjoy all that lay ahead of him. Tyler jumped off the George Washington Bridge in New York City on September 29, 2010, shortly after his roommate streamed videos of Tyler and a male friend having sex on the Internet for the entire world to see. Mortified, humiliated and desperate, he saw no other choice but death. He was 18 years old.

Tyler's suicide placed national attention on the difficulties many gay young people face. Bullying, both in cyber space and in physical space, ostracism, cruelty and fear are the daily companions of many gay teens who live with being different in a world that often seems determined to force everyone to be the same. Many grow up feeling alone, ashamed and unloved. Some, sadly, choose death to escape. I believe that now is the time for all of us to acknowledge, once and for all, that God made some of us straight and some of us gay. I believe that now is the time for all of us to take a stand against the heinous behavior that far too many young people battle on a daily basis simply because of their sexual orientation.

This book is dedicated in memory of Tyler Clementi, and to the many young people just like him who believe that they are alone.

You are not.

INTRODUCTION

The word "no" really bothers me.

The surest way to *get* me to do something is to tell me that I can't do it. Tell me "no," and you've got a fight on your hands. A rebellion. A challenge.

The word bothers me for a lot of reasons, not the least of which stem from growing up in the Deep South, where low "black box" expectations for black kids exclude them from so many things. The black box has had a huge impact on me. I've always been determined to live beyond it, but its very existence has shaped my life, both in front of the camera and behind it. I call the phenomenon the black box because it encompasses a list of expectations and beliefs about black Americans that is as limiting as the four corners of a small box. It's a "no" list for black Americans, men in particular, that, oddly, is sometimes embraced by both blacks and whites. It's something I've never understood and, as I said, something I have actively rebelled against my entire life.

"No" bothers me because it's so often used preemptorily and without justification. When I hear "no," I think automatically "why not?" I want to know the reasons behind the decision. Unfortunately, the reasons usually aren't very good. In fact, they're often terrible excuses. At worse, "no" is often the cover word for a secret. It's the preface to a lie, and a concealer for fear, for shame and lack of will.

My own past has been littered with secrets, and the people around me threw up barriers, shut down questions and offered the word "no" to keep me from finding out the truth.

When I was first approached about writing this book, my answer was "no."

"No" because I have nothing to say.

"No" because I haven't had the career of a Tom Brokaw or of some of the other old school journalists whose life work I greatly admire.

"No" because now is not the time.

Trust me, I had a million reasons *not* to write this book!

Upon further thought, I realized that I was saying "no" for the same reasons I generally despise.

As a journalist, I'm a huge believer in transparency. I don't like communication with a hidden agenda, and I don't like people who conceal things to make themselves look better. Transparency in the process of obtaining information is crucial. Without it, the "news" might as well be called the "spin" or the "opinions" because all bets about its accuracy and objectivity are off. Journalism isn't supposed to be about spin or opinions. It's supposed to be about balance and objectivity. It's about finding the information and putting it out there for the viewer to decide. It's "just the facts, ma'am," to quote the old line from "Dragnet", a TV show that was already in reruns when I was a kid in the late sixties and early seventies.

If a fact is concealed or missing, you get a very different picture of a person or an event than you might have with full disclosure. That's exactly why it matters that journalists tell the truth and present all the facts. If you don't present the viewers with as complete a picture as you can draw, you skew the results. You fail to give the people what they need in order to be able to draw their own conclusions.

In the interest of transparency, it also seems fair for viewers to know something about the people from whom they get their information.

I realized that if I am going to write a book, I will have to face questions regarding my own transparency. How much can I tell? What is relevant to the story and what isn't? If I omit facts about myself, my life, both past and present, that have shaped who I am, will I be violating my personal credo to be myself, and only myself? If I tell everything, will that make me narcissistic?

Will transparency cost me my career?

In writing, I know I'll have to treat myself like a reluctant interviewee and answer some hard questions.

It is a terrifying prospect!

There's a poem by Shel Silverstein that has meant a lot to me over the years. It's called "Listen to the Mustn'ts" and it goes:

> *Listen to the MUSTN'TS, child*
> *Listen to the DON'TS*
> *Listen to the SHOULDN'TS*
> *The IMPOSSIBLES, the WON'TS*
> *Listen to the NEVER HAVES*
> *Then listen close to me—*
> *Anything can happen, child,*
> *ANYTHING can be.*[1]

Thinking of that poem and what it means helped me to decide to move forward with this project and to be as honest and as transparent as possible in these pages. Writing this book represents just one more way I can push the boundaries of "no" and "must not" and reach for the "anythings." I hope that by sharing my personal revelations and experiences, I can also offer inspiration to others.

---

[1] *Where the Sidewalk Ends 30th Anniversary Ed. Poems and Drawings*, Shel Silverstein (HarperCollins, 2004)

Mostly, however, my hope is that this book will remind people everywhere not to accept "no" or "you can't" when they appear in their lives. No matter what happens, or what has happened, know that you are still the captain of your fate. If you choose to live your life as though "no" were not an answer, you might be amazed at where you end up.

Don Lemon
January 2011

PART ONE:

Family and Foundation

CHAPTER 1

A Lesson in Race and Color

On March 1, 1966, the day I was born, Louisiana told me "no" in many ways because I was born black. Fortunately, this little black boy's family didn't get the memo. My family told me "yes," and they affirmed it every day of my life.

My upbringing in Louisiana has shaped who I am in many ways. It gave me an early life full of very hard, very painful and very direct lessons in racism. Think of Louisiana (and much of the South) in the late 1960s and 1970s, the1980s and 1990s, then right on up to and through Hurricane Katrina and the BP oil catastrophe, as ground zero for the status of race and class relations in America.

Everything in Louisiana is about layers. There are layers of race, layers of class, layers of survival, layers of death, and layers of rebirth. To live with these layers is to be a true Louisianan. This state has a depth that is simultaneously beyond words and yet as natural as breathing. How a place can be both other-worldly and completely pedestrian is beyond me; however, Louisiana manages to do it. Louisiana is spooky that way.

My particular little slice of Louisiana is a little town in west Baton Rouge called Port Allen. When I think of Port Allen, the smells of summer seem to fill my nostrils. Summer is heat—the kind that bakes the grass until it almost smells like something fresh out of Mother Nature's oven. Summer is sugar. There was a sugar cane syrup plant near my home and the odor of burnt sugar covered everything. My memories of Port Allen are tinged with that smell. The sun's heat intensified everything. The rivers smelled of fish, and the oak trees grew leaves that were thick and luscious. Even the nearby chemical plants bathed us in their unique stench. It was so hot you could smell the tar melting on the road and under the shingles on the roof.

Port Allen is a mile long from one end to the other. A highway and a parallel railroad track run through its center. When I was growing up there, the highway and the railroad tracks were the racial dividing lines. For the most part, white people lived on one side, and blacks on the other. We shared the grocery store, bank, post office and such.

Somewhere in that town center, maybe at the River Queen, which is the little fast-food joint where my sisters and I would go for burgers and ice cream, is where I first heard a white person call me a "nigger." I hate the word, but I'd rather say it than avoid it with euphemisms like the "N-word." At least it's honest.

One early clue to my journalism destiny was my habit of imitating Peter Jennings and Max Robinson on the *ABC Evening News*. We watched them in the evenings, usually my grandmother and I, since she was my primary caregiver, and I remember repeating "For all of us here at ABC News, good night."

I was the indulged youngest child, and the only boy in a household of women that included my mother, my two older sisters, and my grandmother. Instead of telling me to be quiet, I was encouraged. They thought I was a born entertainer, and smiled at my efforts.

"That baby is gonna be something," my grandmother (we called her "Mame", pronounced "Mah-me") would say proudly.

I believed her, even though by then I already understood that there were some who disagreed.

Traveling with my grandmother gave me some of my first experiences about race, racism and the strange twists on it that color American society. Ironically, some of those experiences are still sometimes relevant today.

Visiting Baton Rouge with Mame was always an interesting experience because of the stares and questions we got.

My grandmother was a very light-skinned woman. So light, in fact, that I thought she was a white woman for many of the earlier years of my life. I'm sure that some of the stares and encounters we had in Baton Rouge were the result of the same confusion. Here was this white woman, holding the hand of an obviously brown-skinned little boy. What were we to each other? People wanted to know. Could she be my teacher? My nanny? Did any blacks in Baton Rouge have *that* kind of money—to hire a white nanny? If not that, what was a light-skinned black woman doing with a child that dark? I'm sure there were some who thought that way. Being properly classified in Louisiana, a place that had invested heavily in the various distinctions of blackness and whiteness to the point of separating octoroons (a person with one-eighth African ancestry, the equivalent of one black great-grandparent and seven white ones) from quadroons (a person with one black grandparent and three white ones), is of the utmost importance. Black people seem to understand these dynamics of coloring and colorism better than white people, but then, for obvious reasons, it has mattered more to us.

If you're looking for a definition, colorism is discrimination in which human beings are accorded differing social treatment based on skin color. Unlike racism, it refers to the discrimination that happens between members of the same race. The preference often gets translated into economic status because opportunities for work are limited or bestowed based upon skin shade. Although colorism can be found across the world, it's something that began in this country when lighter skinned slaves received easier, inside duties than their darker skinned counterparts, who worked in the field. After slavery, lighter skin conferred some blacks a higher status in black communities.[2]

Black America used to be, and perhaps still is, a pigmentocracy, which means that the social hierarchy is based largely on colorism. When I was growing up, Louisiana was ruled by pigmentocracy. I know there are other black communities where colorism has dictated who socializes with whom, what organizations and churches one can belong to, and even where one goes to college, but I suspect that Louisiana is the pinnacle of color consciousness.

It is relevant to say that my experience has been shaped by being a brown-skinned black man—one who is clearly identifiable as an African American. I'm never light enough to "pass" for white, but during the winters, I was light enough to pass the "brown paper bag test." For those of you who are unfamiliar, among blacks of a certain era, the paper bag test was the criterion for who associated with whom. If you were lighter than a brown paper bag, you belonged to one socio-economic class. If you were darker, you belonged to another. If you were light-skinned, you were more likely to have gone to debutante balls and you would attend private or Catholic schools. If you went to college, you might go to one of the more prestigious historically black colleges, like Howard or Southern University.

If you were dark-skinned, on the other hand, you probably weren't going to be going to any deb parties. You were also more likely to attend public school, and if you went to college, you went to schools like Tuskegee Institute.

---

2 *For a simple explanation of colorism, check out: http://en.wikipedia.org/wiki/Colorism*

If your skin shade varied with your level of sun exposure, as mine often did, you were in a no-man's land of acceptance that could switch on and off like a sun lamp. Some days the lighter skinned kids would play with me, and other days they'd look right through me. Some days the darker skinned kids would play with me, and other days they'd tell me to go find some of my light-skinned friends and leave them alone. It was years before white kids became a significant part of my peer group, so these distinctions about skin tone often left me at loose ends among my peers at that time.

This feeling of not fitting in followed me for most of my life. I realize now that it helped me. It made me an astute observer of others and left me free to remain objective.

As a kid, however, it was just lonely, and this was just the beginning. I had yet to have any serious or lasting experiences with white people. I lived in a largely segregated, all black world, and I already felt out of place much of the time.

The lesson I learned from these early experiences is that no matter what "race" or "color" you are, only you can decide what it means to you.

There was another reason I was different, and I soon understood that even in my own family, I was a little out of place. It was my sisters who guided me on my first bit of "investigative reporting," unveiling "Mr. Richardson's secret."

CHAPTER TWO

A Lesson on Secrets

Perhaps one of the reasons that I became a journalist stems from the fact that I had very early lessons with secrets. Those lessons taught me to distrust secrecy almost more than I distrusted anything else.

For the first few years of my life, I didn't know my father as "Dad." I knew him as "Mr. Richardson." My mother was divorced from my sisters' father, but she and my father never married. They were together until he died in 1975, when I was nine, but they couldn't marry.

Mr. Richardson was already married to another woman, a woman who was not my mother. From what I understand, his marriage was a "marriage of convenience." Both he and his wife pursued relationships outside their marriage. At that time in the South, people didn't divorce as readily as they do today. Mr. Richardson was a prominent lawyer in the community, and he and his wife stayed together for the sake of appearances. It was a transparent charade, as Mr. Richardson lived in an apartment at his law office. My mother was his legal secretary. In public, he called her "Ms. Lemon," even though, most days she lived in the office apartment with him.

I remember spending lots of time with Mr. Richardson. My sisters and I would sometimes spend weekends at the apartment with him and Mom. He wasn't the "toss the ball in the front yard" kind of man, but he loved to take me out on the boat or to the health club. He took my whole family on vacations— great vacations. I loved him, but I thought he was just a beloved family friend. I was just a kid, after all, and this was before my innocence was stolen from me.

My sisters, however, knew the real deal. Being tween-aged girls, they were wise beyond their years, or just very interested in adult business. I don't know how they found out. Maybe they always knew. I just remember that one summer day, when we were home alone at Mame's house (she must have gone to the store or the doctor's or something), they got a call from their father in California. I wanted to talk, too, but they discouraged me.

Yma, who was about ten then (five years older than me), crossed her arms over her chest and squinted at me.

"We have to tell you something," she said.

"No, Yma," Leisa said. She was twelve (seven years older) and always the more conservative of the two. Their interactions were often like this—Yma would instigate, and Leisa seemed to talk her out of it, but was actually encouraging her by discouraging her. Leisa shook her head and pursed her lips. "Leave it alone."

"I'm gonna tell him."

"Don't tell that boy that."

"I'm gonna tell him," Yma insisted. She focused her eyes on me and took a deep breath. "You know that Mr. Richardson?"

I nodded.

"Well, he's your *real* daddy," Yma burst out, triumphantly, and then stared at me, waiting to gauge my reaction.

I suppose I might have been shocked, but instead, I felt my chest puffing out with pride. I liked Mr. Richardson. I remember thinking this was wonderful news. It made me feel good. It made me feel special.

"Wow," I said, grinning from ear to ear. "Wow. Really?"

"I think you ought to call him," Yma said, grabbing the big black phone from the side table in the front room.

"You do?" I said.

"No, y'all done enough. Leave it alone," Leisa admonished, which seemed to give Yma permission to push a little further.

Yma ignored her. "You should call him and say 'Hi Daddy.'"

I still remember that number. I still remember my little fingers circling that rotary dial. I don't remember feeling afraid, or feeling like I might even be doing something wrong. I just remember feeling excited by this new information.

It was during the work day and my mother answered. I asked to speak to Mr. Richardson and she didn't question me. When the man answered, without any further prompting by my sisters, I said brightly, "Hi, Daddy."

There was a pause, and then I heard him say to my mother presumably, "Did you hear what he just said? He just called me Dad."

He didn't say anything. I remember him laughing a bit, but my mother said they looked at each other and said, "That baby isn't stupid."

That was that. From then on I called Mr. Richardson "Dad."

Did my sisters get in trouble? Not at all. I think everyone was glad to have the truth in the open. It was healing and good for us all. Of course, I didn't really appreciate the complexities of the situation. I was too young. The important thing was that I knew my father was a man I already loved and respected. It was tremendously empowering and it helped me in ways that I can fully appreciate now as an adult.

I don't want to get on a soapbox, but on the subject of illegitimacy, I feel the need to make at least one small comment. Much is made over the fact that 70% of black children alive today were born out of wedlock. Forty years ago, I might have been counted in that number, but, though my parents weren't married, I had a father who loved me, spent time with me, and supported me emotionally and financially. His influence over my life was immeasurable. My mother still tells the story of how, at no more than the age of three or four, while on vacation with my family, I left the table at a restaurant and started approaching the other diners, interviewing them. This was the late 1960's, and blacks and whites still mixed cautiously. I was a kid, too young to know or care. So there I went, walking up to strangers, asking, "Are you on vacation, too?" "Where are you from?" "Why did you decide to come here?" "When are you leaving?"

"You need to come back here, Don," my mother called. "Leave the people alone." She was nervous for me, afraid I might get some rude white person who didn't feel like having their meal interrupted by an inquisitive black kid.

"Leave him alone," my father said. "Don't teach him to be afraid of people."

Of course, he was right. His encouragement is one of the reasons that I'm confident talking to people of diverse backgrounds and circumstances today.

I almost lost my Dad shortly after I learned of his true identity. Just after I learned about "Mr. Richardson," he and two of his friends were involved in a boating accident. They were out fishing on one of the two big boats that he owned. It was a nice boat, bright white and really big. It was so big that it had a sleeper cabin and everything. Our entire family would spend long, comfortable, lazy summer days on it, navigating the rivers and bayous of Louisiana. It was my favorite boat.

But I digress.

My Dad was an excellent swimmer. He taught me to swim on our fishing trips together during summer vacations when we'd camp on False River, outside of Baton Rouge. I remember starting with those inflatable "floaties" on my arms.

I wasn't with them on the day of the accident, but I remember my grandmother getting the call as she stood in the kitchen. The long cord from the yellow wall phone stretched behind her as she paced back and forth. One hand held the phone as the other moved abruptly from her hip to her mouth.

"Is Richardson okay?" she gasped, clearly upset.

Even though I was just a kid, I was immediately on high alert. Something had happened, and I knew from the look on my grandmother's face and the sound of her voice that it was something bad.

Even though he was an exceptional swimmer, my father always wore a life vest on the boat and demanded that everyone else aboard do the same. Unfortunately, his friends didn't heed his warning.

One of them was smoking a cigarette on board, and somehow the cigarette ignited the boat's gas tank. The boat caught fire and all three of them had to jump into the water and swim for their lives. The boat blew up just as my Dad reached the shore. Unfortunately, his friends didn't make it.

My father called my mother to come pick him up and she called my grandmother, which was the conversation I overheard. Instead of going to the hospital, my dad asked my mother to bring him directly to Mame's house, directly to me. He scooped me up in his arms. I remember it clearly because it was the only time I ever saw fear on his face. He was wearing the pinstriped jumper suit with the snaps up the front that he often wore on the boat, and I remember it was still wet. He wouldn't let me go. Instead, we went out and sat in Mame's long front porch swing and rocked all through the long, hot afternoon until we both fell asleep. Finally, Mame and my mother came to wake us, and to force my dad out of his wet clothes and into a bath and bed. That night, I slept with my dad in Mame's big king sized bed. It was the first time he told me he loved me, but certainly not the last. He told me over and over until the day he died. Imagine if I'd missed out on that.

A father's role is priceless. The marital status of the parents is less of an issue to me. It didn't matter that my parents weren't married. What mattered to me was that they were both *there.* They were both deeply invested in me, my talents, my hopes and my dreams. They gave me their love, their money and their time—three things that all children need.

I didn't realize it then, but having two older sisters was a real advantage, too. I always wanted brothers, probably because I didn't have any, but my sisters offered me a window into how women see the world. They also helped me grow up faster than having brothers would have done, I suspect. They pulled me into the complex realities of how people relate to each other, something I really believe women understand innately better than most men do. They helped me gain understanding some fluency in empathy that, without them, I might never have learned. For that, I am forever grateful.

The "Mr. Richardson affair" was my first experience with secrecy. Then, and even now, I don't understand why that secret was necessary. Looking back, I know that this was my first realization that secrets kill possibilities. This was also the moment that I embarked on my journey towards transparency. Imagine if I'd never known that Mr. Richardson was my father. I would have lost those precious years with him, and that powerful, intimate connection. He died a few years later, and I would have lost forever the chance to call him "Dad" and to hear him call me "son." Those words are irreplaceable. They are priceless.

Of course, there's a difference between privacy and secrecy. I cherish my privacy, but secrecy is something different. "Secrecy" is holding back something critical about one's self out of shame or fear that if it were known, it would cause the person a loss. "Privacy" places boundaries on who has access to some details of one's life. I like to keep certain aspects of my life private from people I don't know well, but they aren't secrets, not by any means.

However, in my life, I have had secrets. Dark, ugly ones that it took me many years to shed light on, and even more years to share, even with those closest to me. I'm resolved not to hold anymore of that shame inside of me and I'm hopeful that, in being honest, I can help others, too.

CHAPTER 3

A Lesson about Loss

I firmly believe that everything in this life happens for a reason and that there are no accidents. It's clear to me now that even the most painful experiences in my life taught me things. While I was going through them, I felt only the hurt.

My father died of diabetes in 1975. My mother worked for my dad for years, but I think he must have had some foreknowledge that he was not long for this world, so he encouraged her to get another job, too, which she did. She went to work for Exxon Chemicals. She had earned her master's degree, and had started work on her doctorate, but the only job she could get in 1974 was as a secretary. My dad helped her buy a house in a newer subdivision that had recently been built in Port Allen. It was in an area that only a few years before had been "whites only" and only a few black families had homes there.

Our house was only a few years old when we bought it, but my mother wanted to make changes. She was expanding the den and adding a patio. In the process of the remodeling, we think a roofing tack got stuck in my dad's shoe and, because of the poor circulations in his extremities caused by diabetes, he kept wearing the shoe without feeling the tack sticking into his big toe again and again and aggravating the wound. Over several agonizing months, blood poisoning cost him first his toe, then his foot, then his leg up to the knee. Finally, on September 3, 1975, he died in the hospital when a blood clot stopped his heart. To this day, the fall brings me a mild case of depression. It reminds me of my dad's death and the end of my life with him.

I didn't get to see my dad much in the months before he died. First, because he didn't want us children to see him as he lost pieces of himself and grew sicker and sicker. Secondly, children under a certain age weren't allowed in to visit, even during visiting hours.

I did visit him at his office apartment one weekend. My mom pulled me aside as she was about to clean the area around his amputated toe with a salt bath and said, "Don't say anything about Daddy's toe. Don't make a big deal over it, okay?" She knew her curious son well. So did my dad.

So when Mom removed the bandages, my dad brought up the subject first, telling me it was just temporary and that Daddy would be okay. I remember staring at the place where his toe had been and feeling the overwhelming urge to magically restore it with a blink of my eyes or a twitch of my nose, like on those TV shows *I Dream of Jeannie* or *Bewitched.* Even through his noticeable pain and embarrassment, he explained every move my mom made as she swabbed the spot.

"First, Mommy has to carefully unwrap Daddy's bandage, and I have to be still while she cleans up Daddy's foot. Wanna hold the bandage for Mama?" he said.

Mom, with a half smile on her face, but still serious, said, "Alright, boys, let's get Dad in the tub."

The very last time I saw my dad was a few weeks later when he came to our house in Port Allen to spend the weekend. By then, his entire foot was gone. He didn't do much walking, and when he did, it was done carefully, with the assistance of my mother and some giant, pine-colored wooden crutches. A few weeks later, he was gone.

My sister, Yma, and I were cooking pecan candy when my mom's friend, Cal, came over to deliver the news. She was sobbing and hugged me a long time. I cried, but I didn't understand exactly why. I didn't understand the permanence of it. Cal, my mother and my aunt (my mom's sister) spent the next several hours going back and forth to my dad's law office apartment, removing all evidence that she had ever lived there. It took many trips back and forth in Mom's old brown Chevy station wagon and Dad's white Lincoln Continental to retrieve all of Mom's designer dresses, ball gowns, shoes, jewelry, perfumes, photographs, toiletries and love letters. A few weeks later, my mom had to return the Lincoln Continental to the law office and shepherd my dad's wife through the unfinished business, paperwork and court cases. She had to give her the safe combinations and the keys. I don't know how she did it, but she did, never letting on the pain she was experiencing by having to pretend that my dad was her beloved boss and nothing more.

After my dad's funeral, his wife invited our entire family to her home, along with others in the community, so that everyone could say their final goodbyes to Mr. Richardson. She, my mom and my dad's mom (the grandmother I never got to know) sat and chatted in her big, white, stately home, not far from my dad's office.

My "other grandmother" kept staring at me as I mingled with guests and scurried around my dad's big house. Finally, just before we left that house and the life we had shared with him for good, my other grandmother looked right at me and blurted out, loud enough for all to hear:

"Boy, you look just like Richardson. Are you sure you're not Richardson's son?" Those were her exact words.

I was tempted to answer. My mom kept still and quiet. My dad's wife quickly and awkwardly guided the conversation to another subject, and just like that, our family started a new life. No more amazing Christmas trips. No more family vacations. No more weekends at our summer camp. No more weekend boating expeditions. No more Friday night family dinners at the apartment. No more backyard barbecues. No more fancy cars. No more expensive hotels. No more fatherly advice or discipline. For my sisters and my grandmother, no more Mr. Richardson. For me, no more Daddy.

My mom still cries for and dreams about the man she calls the "love of her life" and the best man she ever knew. After he died, she was deeply depressed as she grieved. She literally shut down. She shut herself away from people, and started spending most of the time she wasn't at work alone in her dark bedroom. This went on for at least six months. I remember climbing into bed with her at night, snuggling close, trying to comfort her. I couldn't.

I remember her working in the front yard, sobbing. She hated to be caught with her emotions so raw. She just wanted to be alone with her feelings. In order to distract me and my sisters, she would often hand us money, and encourage us to go somewhere, anywhere, so she could be alone with her pain. Somehow, she pulled herself out of it, which is yet another testament to her strength.

My father's friends wasted no time in hovering around her, each attempting to become the new man in her life. It would have been funny if it hadn't been so pathetic.

ೲ

Until we moved to the new house, we had lived with my grandmother, and her constant presence had offered me some protection, but not enough to keep one particular teenager away. On weekends, my father had been my saving grace. When he died, and my mother and grandmother were less present in my life, I was vulnerable in new ways. What had started at my grandmother's house as a rare, but painful, experience became a sad and frequent part of my life.

I was 30 years old before I even told my mother what happened to me. The shame, the confusion, and the sense of humiliation runs that deep and becomes that twisted. Even though some experts estimate that nearly a third of all adults were molested as children, they can't be sure. Childhood sexual abuse often goes unreported and unpunished. Most children who are molested know their abusers, which was the case for me.

He was a teenage neighbor, and a contemporary of one of my older sisters. I was only five years old at the time. It continued for years, and I wasn't the only victim. This individual would be known today as a predator. He and several of his friends preyed on the smaller kids in the neighborhood, taking advantage of our size and our fear of them to keep us quiet. Of course, they had an even more powerful weapon than that. They convinced us that we were doing something wrong, too. Telling on them would be telling on ourselves.

You want salacious details?

Use your imagination. I'm not giving a play by play, as that's not healthy for me at this point in my life. I will say that everything that you can imagine actually happened, only the pain, fear and humiliation are all worse than you can possibly imagine, unless you've actually lived it yourself.

After that, I knew I was different, and not just because of the color composition of my family, or because I had a different father than my sisters. I had been *made* different. Warped.

I never told anyone, at least not until 20 years later when the consequences were entirely different. I don't know if anyone else told, but I doubt it. As I said, the shame goes that deep. Even as a child, I sensed that my accusation wouldn't be met with concern and support. I sensed that I would be perceived as "tainted" and that the entire matter would be quickly swept under the community rug, never to be addressed.

As an adult, however, my experience is something I feel compelled to share for several reasons. The first is that it's a part of who I am and what I've become. It's another experience that makes me do what I do, think what I think, believe what I believe and see the world the way that I do. To hide it would not only be disingenuous of a person who has said repeatedly, in forum after forum, that I believe in transparency, but it would also mean that I'm still playing the "shame game." Fear and intimidation are also the tools of abusers. I'm not playing the "fear game" either.

I probably wouldn't have addressed the whole issue of my own experience with childhood sexual abuse during the context of a news story, but the accusations against Bishop Eddie Long, and the things the members of his congregation said in his defense, triggered me.

I had met Bishop Long two years before, in 2008, on a special panel discussion for CNN called "Black Men in the Age of Obama." The panelists included me, Dr. Farrah Gray, and Bishop Eddie Long, lead pastor of the New Birth Missionary Baptist Church, a mega-church in Atlanta, Georgia. The conversation ranged from family values, to education, to economics and relationships.

In September 2010, four young men, very young, with the average age being 17, just over the age of consent, alleged that Long plied them with gifts, money and trips in exchange for sexual contact. I contacted Bishop Long, but he declined an opportunity to discuss those allegations in an interview on CNN. Instead, I interviewed members and former members of his congregation about the Bishop, the young men's allegations and their thoughts about the charges.

The story was like a trigger for me. I suspect it was partly because I was working on this book, and had been thinking a lot about my own experiences with abuse. They say, "You're not gay if you do this." It's one of the ways that abusers convince their victims that no one will ever believe them. How does one go from watching TV with a guy to performing sexual acts with him? It doesn't seem like something that flows naturally, unless there's something wrong with you. Unless you're some kind of deviant. Those are the circumstances sexual predators, pedophiles and abusers use. They are the reason more and more victims don't come forward.

When one church member said words to the effect of he didn't believe the accusations because the kids were basically just invited to watch TV and that seemed completely harmless, I spoke out.

I said, "I am admitting something that I have never admitted on TV. I, too, was a victim of a pedophile who was much older than I was as a child. The words they used, like "you're not gay if you do this", are some of the same things my abuser said to me."

In a way, I surprised myself. It was completely spontaneous, and I had no idea I was going to say it, but having said it, I wasn't really concerned about the reaction. As I've said, I don't play the shame game. It happened, it was appropriate and relevant to the interview I was conducting and I didn't feel that mentioning my experience as an explanation for why Bishop Long's explanations might be suspect hijacked the conversation. I didn't feel like those few sentences had made the conversation about me, instead of one about the pastor and the allegations against him.

I wasn't concerned about what the feedback would be after the interview. I've learned that there are always both positive and negative reactions to almost everything I say on the air, and I expected this would be no different. However, it was. It was different because I've yet to really receive any negative reactions to making this revelation.

I started getting tweets and texts from viewers around the country, thanking me for my courage, sharing their own experiences with molestation and sexual abuse, and delving more deeply into the statistics about abuse and its costs to our society.

This was a reminder for me that transparency is crucial in journalism, and that who I am and what I've experienced as a person both play roles in the way I ask questions. I think it's important for journalists to be open and honest when they've had experiences that are relevant to the issues of the day. I think this approach helps to neutralize the perception of bias.

As I write these words, Bishop Long's case hasn't been litigated. I don't know if he's guilty or innocent, and I certainly don't mean to suggest either possibility with anything I've said or written. That's for a jury to decide, but to the extent that my experiences can help us all have a more open and honest discussion about childhood sexual abuse, I don't regret anything that I've said.

It's time to shed some light on these problems and admit to them in the black community and in the world at large. It's time to acknowledge the cost of silence, both in dollars and in human capital. Did you know, for example, that according to the United States Department of Justice, 15% of the men in prison right now were abused as children? Also, according a recent report released by the National Institute on Drug Abuse, abused children are more likely to end up abusing drugs than their counterparts who were not molested. Both of these things ultimately happened to the boy who molested me. He was in and out of jail, on and off drugs, and went on to lead a deeply-troubled life. I have no doubt that someone else had done to him what he did to me in an endless, violent cycle. His friends faced a similar fate, or jail and substance abuse. One of them has HIV/AIDS, or so I hear. Understandably, these are men who, now, as adults, I have no contact with.

Discussing this topic in this book is not about providing you, the reader, with salacious details or achieving some kind of cleansing therapy for myself. My hope is that, by being forthright on this subject, I can continue the national dialogue on this painful, ugly topic. The facts are pretty clear on the damage that childhood sexual abuse does to our population. In fact, according a report commissioned by the Pew Research Trust, experts estimate that child molestation costs the United States nearly $104 billion a year in correctional facilities, in health care costs related to substance abuse, and in mental health issues and diseases. The human cost is incalculable.

I don't know how it is that, unlike the teenager who molested me, I'm not in jail, not an addict, and not perpetrating similar crimes on others. I can attribute it to the other influences in my life, such as a loving family, a lifelong goal, a sense of faith that things would get better, and the heartfelt belief that I could change my fate. But probably, even those things don't explain it. It truly is one of the many instances of my life where nothing but grace explains why for one child a horrible circumstance becomes a motivator, and for another, it ends as a fast track to the penitentiary.

The teen who abused me wasn't just any neighborhood kid. He was the son of one of my mother's friends. In many ways, our circumstances were similar, but I guess, there were also important, life altering differences.

In the end, two things ultimately became my saving grace. The first was St. Francis Xavier, the Catholic school I attended from kindergarten through eighth grade. Boarding the school bus every day and leaving my Port Allen community to join kids with backgrounds completely different from my own, took me away from both my abuser and a community of silence. This opportunity to escape completely changed the trajectory of my life. It took me away from the public schools in Port Allen, where my abuser and his friends preyed on the other kids in my neighborhood. The second savior came in the form of my step-father, who, when he and my mother married, moved our entire family out of that community.

The loss of my father and the loss of my innocence while I was still a young child gave me a powerful gift of empathy for people who are going through traumatic experiences. This gift has served me well in my work and in my life. The spirit that guides us, whether you call him God, Jesus, Allah or something else, brings us our challenges for specific reasons. My familiarity with loss, firsthand, makes me a better reporter and a better person.

CHAPTER 4

A Lesson in Trust

L ouisiana is a place of sex and good times. New Orleans, in particular, has this reputation, and has had it since the days of slavery when white slave owners would bring their black mistresses there to "vacation" openly. Along with the "rolling good times," there have always been dark places. I know some of these dark places.

I might easily have shrunk under the weight of shame and guilt associated with years of abuse, had fate not intervened, providing me and my family with a lesson in learning to trust and love again.

After my father died, so did his financial support. My mother needed to make extra money to support us all, and the only way to do that was to work, not in the Exxon office, but out in the oil refineries. This was shift work, and men's work, at the time. There was only one other woman on the job site, and there wasn't even a women's bathroom. It wouldn't be unfair to say that my mother, in addition to her other strengths and achievements, was something of a pioneer of equal opportunities for women, when she accepted this job.

My stepfather worked at the refinery, and one day he saw this fine, black woman and he said to his co-workers, "Who is *that*?"

When he asked her out, my mother sat me and my sisters down and asked us how we'd feel about her dating again. I remember wanting to know about this man, and wanting to meet him. I wanted to make sure he wasn't like my dad's old friends who were being shady and always trying to hit on her. She practically glowed when she talked about how handsome he was, and how he drove the cutest truck. I wanted to see the man who had my mother all girlish and excited just to make sure he was on the up and up. I remember telling her that it was fine, and that I wanted to her to go out and have fun. In my heart, I knew that even if he was a decent guy, their dating would only be okay as long as he didn't try to replace my dad.

The first time I met him, I thought he was confident and strong. The more time I spent with him, the more I saw that he was nothing like what he pretended to be. He tried to be tough, but he really wasn't. He was just as gentle, scared and uncertain as I was, just as we all are behind our facades and our defenses. I can only imagine how he must have felt, realizing he was falling in love with a woman who had three half-grown children. I was 11 and my sisters were 16 and 18. He knew how much we had all loved my dad. He knew that my sisters kept in touch with their father in California. He must have been terrified of our rejection and also worried that a blended family wouldn't work.

He loved my mother very dearly and passionately, and he wanted little more than to be around her and be close to her. My sisters were older and already on the paths of their own lives. He wisely chose to be kind and friendly toward them, but not to insist on more. I was younger, and also the only boy, and he tried his best to bond with me.

The only problem was that he, like many men of his generation, really didn't know *how*. It wasn't yet the time when men were free to reveal their gentler, more affectionate sides, and I think my step-father felt constrained by his generation's definitions of "manliness." Just the same, he really wanted to reach out to me and to make a connection, so he settled for the easiest and most expedient way. He gave me money, bought me a car and provided for me financially in every way.

Now before you miscast as me as simply a grasping and avaricious pre-teen, let me clarify. I appreciated his financial support, as most teens would, but I also grew to love him for the man he was. I understood him. We genuinely liked each other. We were both stubborn, free spirits who had a strong sense of our selves. He was also incredibly shrewd about our relationship. He knew

I was the apple of my mother's eye, and that if I was happy, she would be happy, too.

I'm aware that I sound spoiled, materialistic and over-indulged. I plead guilty to that charge to a certain degree. However, I avoided narcissism and arrogance, thanks to my sisters, who had a deep awareness of my limitations and no compunction about sharing their awareness with me. My sisters were the ones who kept me from becoming a self-indulgent Mama's boy. They spoiled me, too, but they also grounded me.

"Oh, so Donny's got a *car* now," they'd tease. "He thinks he's all *that.*"

Their laughter reminded me that possessions didn't make me any better than anyone else. Like good sisters everywhere, they laughed and teased me for everything that I thought made me "cool" or "smooth," from my haircut to my wardrobe to my school activities.

They also put me to work in their lives. I babysat Leisa's first child, balanced her checkbook, helped her set up her savings plan, and bought her clothes. I've helped Yma in similar ways. To this day, both are like old friends with whom I can sit and talk about anything over a glass of wine. I can imagine what they'll say when this book is released—"Did you have to tell *all* our family secrets, Mr. News Man?" We'll all laugh. We remain close.

ᴔ

It was a fast romance. My mom and stepfather married in the living room of our home in Port Allen in August 1976. After the wedding, we moved to a neighborhood near Southern University called "Park Vista." It wasn't far from where my dad's offices had been, but it was in North Baton Rouge. It was only twelve miles from Port Allen. Sixteen minutes in the car, but a world away from the years of torment I'd endured in Port Allen.

Park Vista was a community of "uppity black people," to use the vernacular of the times. These were the black engineers who worked at Exxon, and the Southern University professors. They were the talented tenth that W.E.B. DuBois[3] wrote of. My stepdad was a pipefitter, not nearly the sort for Park Vista. He had survived a serious accident at Exxon, falling seven floors down to the ground on a refining elevator. He received a substantial personal injury settlement, so he worked when he wanted to. His first wife had been a university professor and that's how he ended up in Park Vista. When he and my mother decided to marry, it was decided that my mother would keep, but shutter, her house in Port Allen and move into his home. This moved me across town and out of the reach of my abuser forever.

There was a great deal of curiosity about us when we moved in. The good people of Park Vista wanted to know who we were and if we were their "kind." We were, and we weren't. The emphasis they placed on education and the pride they took in their property were admirable. Like in many suburban neighborhoods across America, lawn care in Park Vista was a competitive sport,

---

3 *William Edward Burghardt Dubois (1868-1963) was a civil rights activist, one of the founders of the NAACP and another personal hero of mine. He wrote about role of the "Talented Tenth"—the educated African American upper class—in racial uplift in his 1903 work "The Souls of Black Folk."*

as was the accumulation of wealth and the need to keep up with the Joneses. Along with mansions, manicured lawns, and clean cars, Park Vista was loaded with pretense.

There were issues boiling beneath the surface, including money troubles, addiction, and kids who were dropping out and doing drugs. These facts were never admitted to. It was the black version of *Mad Men*, right down to the furniture and decorations.

Some of their homes were gigantic with swimming pools and the perfect accoutrements. Every day, at six in the evening, the sprinklers would come on. Weekend car washing was required, and many families had a "cleaning lady." My sister's college professor lived next door, and the physician lived around the corner. They were the black upper middle class. There were some of those families in Port Allen, but Park Vista was where they lived in high concentration.

My dad, Mr. Richardson, had been upper middle class. He probably could have bought and sold some of these people. While he was alive, we had never wanted for anything, but even then, we didn't live the kind of life that was just "every day" for the residents of Park Vista, so with residency, we had to step up our game.

When my mom and stepfather got married, my mom had to join the social club. Every club member was responsible for hosting the membership at her home at some point during the year. When my mother's turn came, she sprang into action. The house had to be spotless, floors Johnson-waxed and manually buffed to high shine, and every speck and crumb swept, polished or scrubbed. Our house was cleaned until you could smell the chemicals clashing in the air. Then, with the cleaning complete, my mom made an elaborate pot of gumbo, bought a fancy new dress and had her hair done. On the day of the party, the kids made themselves scarce—until the adults all got tanked. Then I commandeered the record player and played songs from the "Saturday Night Fever" soundtrack like the *Bee Gees'* "Stayin' Alive." Then I played *The Commodores* or *The Isley Brothers or The Gap Band.* Don't forget Donna Summer and *The O'Jays*—it was music to move to at that time, and it still is.

Several of my friends from St. Francis Xavier lived nearby, and I still traveled by bus to and from my old school. After nine years in Catholic school, I'd had enough. I wanted to do something different. I loved my school, but we prayed constantly—before classes, before lunch, and before going home at the end of the day. We wore uniforms that suppressed my sartorial style and I was tired of it. I wanted more freedom. I wanted to wear my own clothes. I wanted to leave the building without saying a prayer. Don't get me wrong, I have deep faith, even if I'm not what most would describe as "religious." I know there's a higher power for good that keeps this world spinning, but at the age of 14, I was less concerned about my immortal soul and more concerned about having the freedom to dress the way I wanted.

It was 1980. Jimmy Carter had lost his bid for re-election to Ronald Reagan and there were still American hostages being held at the American Embassy in Iran. *Dallas* was one of the most popular shows on television. So were *Benson* and *Taxi*.

Fashion was making a dramatic shift from flowing ethnic styles and the disco excess of the 1970s to a more tailored look. Preppy was in and I was all over it.

I was a teenager, learning to trust myself and wanting to venture into new territory. In spite of how happy I was at St. Francis Xavier, I felt I was ready for a new experience. I decided I wanted to go to public high school.

My parents and I talked about it. They warned me it would be a big change, and that it might be more difficult than I thought to make this transition. I would hear none of it. I wanted to go public high school. I yearned for freedom, individuality and change.

Mom and I went shopping. I bought so many clothes in preparation for my freshman year of high school that I never wore the same thing twice that entire year. It was ridiculous, of course, but in my mind, clothes were all that I needed to navigate the bridge between my sheltered private school and the wider world of public school. I was such a clothes horse, even then, and I still am. When I have time, I prowl vintage stores. I often have things custom-made because the fit is always superior to anything you buy off the rack. These are among the many lessons I got from my grandmother, who knew the value of classic, well-made clothing.

That summer, I covered my anxieties with shopping. I knew that when school started I'd be looking good, but as the summer wore on, I began to regret my decision to leave the security of my friends and my familiar surroundings at St. Francis Xavier.

By the time mid-August rolled around, I was sure I was making the worst decision of my young life.

I had all the typical adolescent fears—that I wouldn't know anyone, and I'd have no friends and end up the ultimate outsider. My fears completely overtook me. After filling my closets with secular clothes, I went to my mother and my stepfather and begged them to see if I could go to Redemptorist High School, which was a Catholic school.

They tried, but by then, there were no vacant slots. My parents also contacted Catholic High School, an all-boys school, but there weren't any openings there either. Even Baton Rouge High School, the public magnet school, was full. I had no choice. I was going to the public high school. It was complete culture shock, for all of the reasons I expected and a few that I didn't.

My stepfather, and my beloved former school, had given me new tools to trust myself in unfamiliar environments. It's a lesson I've called upon time and time again in my life, both in my career and in my personal life. Learning to open your heart to trust others is always an act of faith, but learning to reach inside and trust yourself is a life lesson that is priceless.

CHAPTER 5

A Lesson in Diversity

As I mentioned previously, colorism in the black community shaped me, but it wasn't until I was in high school that I really confronted the notions of race and racism, both my own and that of others. The lessons I learned about myself, about interacting with people of other ethnicities, about the common values and interests that ultimately formed my friendships and the humanity we all share, have influenced much of how I interact with others in my adult life. Until I went to high school, however, I had none of those understandings.

You have to appreciate what I had come from. Except for a year in pre-school at a program run by the Mt. Zion Baptist Church, St. Francis Xavier was the only school experience I had ever known. It was extremely small and I had gone to school with the same 25-30 kids since kindergarten. I knew those kids quite well and was completely comfortable with them. I also knew all the nuns and all the teachers. I knew Sister Ann Elise, the first principal, and her successor, Sister Patricia Ann. I knew the daily routine—at the start of the day we'd line up outside on the little playground attached to the school, then file into our classrooms. There were announcements, and then every morning we'd stand to pray, then stand for the "Pledge of Allegiance" and remain standing for the "Star Spangled Banner." There would be lessons, then a prayer before lunch, and another one afterwards, before we started our lessons for the afternoon. There was daily choir class where we all learned to sing. At the end of the day, there was a final prayer before we filed out of the classroom to meet our parents in their cars, or catch our bus. I first learned the importance of order and discipline from the nuns, and it's a lesson I'm grateful for to this very day.

On Friday, there was Mass. My family wasn't Catholic, but I participated fully in every ceremony. In fact, my first grade teacher, Ms. Hebert (pronounced in the French way "A-bear"), encouraged me to read, to work hard on my assignments and to develop the habits of a good student. She also encouraged me to stand up and do the readings from the scripture, which are usually done by members of the congregation, or lay readers during the Catholic worship service. So, from the tender age of six, I was standing up in front of the whole school, reading scripture. Usually, it went well, but not always.

My sister, Yma, who attended St. Francis for a short while before being home schooled due to scoliosis surgery, used to brag about me doing the readings. "My little brother is going to read the scripture at Mass on Friday," she'd tell her friends. "My little brother's gonna be in the school play." Of course, sometimes she'd regret having made so much of my "performances." Like the time I forgot the word "takes" in the scripture "Jesus takes care of his sheep." "Takes" isn't a particularly difficult word, but I was in first grade at the time and for some reason, even though the word was on the piece of paper in front of me, I just couldn't figure it out. Mrs. Hebert tried to help me. I remember her mouthing the words from the pews, but I'm not much of a lip reader, and I was nervous and scared that I would be in trouble for not remembering the word. Finally, Ms. Hebert came up and read the word to me in a low voice, "Jesus takes care of His sheep." I blurted it out in relief and hurried back to my seat.

It was an embarrassing incident and I vowed that it wouldn't happen again. I started to work on training my memory. Every year, St. Francis Xavier had a big Christmas pageant, and every year I tried out. I always got a part and I usually got a pretty *big* part, simply because when it came time to audition I had memorized the entire play. Not just the parts I was auditioning for, but *all of it*. I'd go to the auditions, stand up and just start rattling off the play. The teachers were really impressed, and I confess,

I loved to show off. Thinking about how amazed everyone was gave me the incentive to learn it all.

It just so happens that having a good memory, and being able to retain lots of information, is a skill that has ultimately served me very well in my chosen profession. It also helps that I loved to read. I learned math, but I struggled with it. I was able to memorize the basics, such as the repetitions of addition, subtraction and multiplication, but by the time I hit division, I was in trouble. I just didn't like it.

I remember the exact moment that I fell behind in math and never caught up. I was in the fourth grade and I came down with a terrible flu. I had a high fever, and I couldn't walk, eat or even swallow. My mom and grandmother took me to the doctor, who immediately put me on a battery of medication and strict bed rest. I missed two weeks of school. When I began to feel better, Yma helped me with all my homework assignments, including math. We almost finished my entire math text book, but when I returned to school two weeks later, my math teacher was so indignant that I had completed the work before the rest of the students, and without her assistance, that she tore up my math workbook and removed me from the advanced math group. After that, I was discouraged and afraid of math. I was good at performing, reading and writing. I was so good, in fact, that sometimes teachers accused me of having someone else write my papers because I understood the flow of words so well.

You know that saying that "It takes a village to raise a child?" St. Francis Xavier was my village. It was a real family, and a real community. From the nuns to the cafeteria ladies, to the students and the parents, the teachers and everyone else, St. Francis Xavier nurtured me. It was an amazing institution. I wish for every child that kind of experience, an educational experience where you truly feel that everyone is committed to your success. I never pledged a fraternity, but I would imagine it is the same kind of experience of community. It's a family that's made, not by blood, but forged by common dedication. St. Francis Xavier will always be the epitome of "community" to me. I still miss the people there every day. Not a day goes by that I don't think about some of them and wonder how they are doing. I even dream I'm back there, especially at that old, old church. They've since built a new one, but it just isn't the same. The old church had a *heart*, and I felt it beat every time I stood inside. I can still remember the sounds of the school, and the metal railings of the fence surrounding it rattling in the wind. I can still remember the smell of the old hallways and classrooms and the aroma of fresh bread baking in the cafeteria below the Performance Hall.

Though I ultimately grew to appreciate its lessons, too, I have none of the same memories of Baker High School.

When I attended Baker High, in the town of Baker, just north of North Baton Rouge, it was a predominantly white school, perhaps only 25% black. It had been fully integrated only a few years before. The school was in the same part of town as the local headquarters of the Ku Klux Klan, which was daunting. For the first time in my sheltered life, I was in an environment where I was a minority.

It was an awkward experience. I struggled to fit in and to find friends. I remember feeling like I was faking it all the time in an effort to be liked, but I think most teenagers feel that way. Popularity and being liked are extremely important to a teenager, more so than they are as he grows older. These days, I don't worry about this at all, which might seem surprising considering that I'm in a field where Nielsen ratings and your TV Q rating (your popularity to the viewing audience) sometimes dictate your career. Quite honestly, none of this concerns me. I guess I've learned that there will always be people who like you as well as people who don't. Worrying about being liked changes how willing you are to take risks. At least it did for me.

When I was a kid, I was uninhibited and a born performer. As a teenager, I became more hesitant. I still wanted to be a journalist, but I stopped doing my Peter Jennings' imitation. In elementary school, I used to take my family's super 8 mm camera and go around interviewing friends and relatives, making little vignettes. I stopped doing this, too, until college, when my parents bought a VHS camera. In the self-awareness that is a part of adolescence, I suddenly realized there were no people who looked like me on TV. No, I take that back. There was JJ Walker and there was Rerun, but they were caricatures. They weren't me.

I started thinking of myself differently, and began focusing on the immediate need to make friends and be liked. I *was* liked, and in a way my shopping sprees worked to my advantage. I came to be known as the kid with all the clothes, and I incorporated a personality to match. Eventually, I was voted "Most Liked" by my senior class.

As good as all this sounds, there were definite tensions. I got compliments on my clothes and sometimes even my looks, though I never thought of myself, and still don't think of myself, as particularly good-looking. Attractive, yes. Good looking? Not so much. Several of the white kids I talked with at school would never have invited me to their homes or been caught at mine, so the lines of socialization and segregation were still quite clear.

Perhaps things might have been a bit easier if I'd known the black kids at Baker High School a little better. All my friends had gone to Catholic school and were still there. I was a stranger to most of the black students at Baker High School, who had gone to public schools together since kindergarten. With my sheltered, parochial school habits and ways, I probably seemed pretty odd to them.

I was a kid who still lived in the shadow of a terrible secret. I don't think I understood it fully at the time, but deep down inside, I never felt like I was "just one of the kids" at Baker. My experiences had already made me something else. I was someone a little apart from others.

There was also the issue of my unfamiliarity with white people, which only added to my heaping mounds of insecurities—kind of like the cherry on top. This was the first time I'd gone to school with white kids, and for me it was strange.

Like many high schools around the country, both then, and unfortunately, probably now, Baker High was a school where the black kids and white kids divided, each group hanging only with their own. Since I didn't know the black kids any better than I did the white kids, I didn't know who to hang with. As a result, I was alone much of the time. You might even describe me in those years as "a loner," which has actually been a constant theme in my life.

✧

St Francis Xavier didn't have a Physical Education class. It was a small private school, and there wasn't room for a gym. Occasionally, we went to the community recreation center to play basketball, but not on a regular basis. In my final years, the school hired a gym teacher who put together a rag-tag basketball team. We were horrible. Imagine all of us sheltered Catholic school kids with little prior physical training going up against middle school kids who had been shooting hoops all their lives. It was worse than *The Bad News Bears*, and probably even funnier to watch.

Having a "gym class" was something new to me. I'd barely been around white people at all and I certainly hadn't been strutting around the locker room naked with them, so it was weird. I didn't want to get undressed, wear the silly shorts, and play games that I didn't know how to play. My discomfort was probably obvious and I'm sure it made me seem even stranger to my fellow students. I tried to follow the gym teacher's instructions. I was, and still am, naturally athletic, but I wasn't exactly good at any sports. In fact, I hadn't had much exposure to most sports and when it came time to do a unit on wrestling, for all kinds of reasons, I was pretty grossed out by the entire concept of having some smelly, sweaty guy on top of me. It was weird being close to people who smelled different and had different hair.

As it turned out, I was pretty good at wrestling. I had been involved with a Baton Rouge Police Mentor program that had gotten us kids involved with running, so I was fast and I was strong. Although I had absolutely no experience with wrestling, in my freshman year I made it to the final round at the state tournament. I wish I could say it was because I developed an appreciation for the sport, but it was mostly because I was embarrassed by the form-fitting wrestling tights and I didn't want to be under any smelly, sweaty guys ever again.

After we finished the unit on wrestling, I had no interest in joining the wrestling team, or pursuing it any further. I might have spent my entire high school career at sixes and sevens, had it not been for two very different people—Shellette Wade and Jon Dupre.

Shellette Wade was a beautiful, brown-skinned girl who rode the same school bus as I did to Baker High, until we both got cars during our freshman year. She wasn't as well-off as the kids who lived in Park Vista, but she became my first real friend. We liked each other and went out occasionally, but we weren't romantic. I would say we were each other's "back up date," someone to hang out with when there weren't more intriguing prospects. She had gone to the area public schools since kindergarten and she knew all of the black kids. As we grew closer, her friends became my friends.

Jon Dupre couldn't have been more different from Shellette. He was a senior, a white southern good old boy who I met during my sophomore year. Jon was a rebel. He had a big blonde Mohawk, drove a huge, dirty truck to school, wore faded, peg-legged Levi's and came from a blue-collar family. He was quite a character. We had a business class together. We were also in a club called the Interact Club, a junior Rotary club that I was invited to join by my biology teacher, Mr. Noble. Jon's father was a single dad, raising Jon and his little brother alone after their mother left them. He invited me to his house for a sleepover and his father told me that the Grand Wizard of the local KKK chapter lived a few houses down. When I told my mother, she refused to let me sleep there anymore because she was afraid for me. As a result, most of the time, Jon came to my house. His dad and younger brother even came to dinner with my family and had a ball.

Since he was such a rebel, Jon wasn't like the rest of the kids, and neither was his family. He introduced me to all his friends and they, too, became my friends. In the end, I became friends with the white kids at Baker High School more quickly than I became friends with the black kids. Before high school was over, I had friends from so many different backgrounds that my mom and I used to joke that I was like the United Nations, with a friend who represented almost every country!

I know it sounds strange in the 21st century when the Internet and other technology has shrunk our world dramatically and we're able to interact with people all over the globe with nothing more than our cell phones or our broadband connections, but in the 1980s, had it not been for Baker High School, I would have had very little interaction with people who looked different than I did. It was even less likely that I would have called someone with a different skin tone "friend."

As nervous as I was about going to Baker High School initially, the experience gave me a tremendous gift. It forced me to become a much more well-rounded person than I would have been if I'd spent my high school years at an all-black school. I learned about how other people lived, and this broadened my horizons in ways that staying in my all-black enclave never would have done. I learned that people are all the same, and this knowledge has aided me immeasurably in my life.

I believe in this lesson, and I've been lucky enough to meet people all over the world who confirm the basic humanity of all of us, no matter what color our skin, what languages we speak, or what creeds we believe in.

Sometimes there were black kids who wondered why I was friends with so many white kids. This was the first time I really came into contact with the idea of the "black box." Little did I know, the black box and I would have a long and interesting career together.

CHAPTER 6

A Lesson on the "Black Box"

Again and again in my life, I've run up against those who have limited ideas about what and who black Americans are, and sometimes expressions of those limitations have come from black people themselves. I call these beliefs the black box and I got my first real black box lessons in high school.

I wouldn't say that Baker High was fraught with racial tensions because, for the most part, the black and white students got along civilly. Black and white kids spoke to each other and acknowledged each other. There weren't any fights, but people did say insensitive things to each other, which escalated the level of distrust between the races. In my opinion, these insensitivities were largely because the two communities didn't mix beyond the surface level. Both blacks and whites had formed beliefs about each other based in ignorance, stereotypes and fear.

As a black man who had white friends, I got some push-back reaction from the other black kids. "Why are you friends with all those white people?" they'd ask me. "Why are you hanging around them all the time?"

My response of "They're my friends," was met with a certain level of suspicion. As I've said, whites and blacks didn't really interact that way in Baton Rouge in the 1980s. Some of those tensions still remain in Louisiana today. When Hurricane Katrina devastated New Orleans in 2005, we saw the residue of centuries of suspicion between white and black communities that still have very little to do with each other. Both races have created an idea of what it means to be "black," and those ideas can have some pretty dangerous consequences.

As a high school student, I was on the receiving end of assumptions from blacks and whites about what it meant to be "black." Now, almost 30 years later, I'm still having those experiences. The difference now is that I'm more comfortable challenging anyone's assumptions about how I define my blackness than I was as a teenager.

With the wisdom and distance of adulthood, I've come to understand that the "black box" serves a dual purpose. It offers safety and community for Black Americans, but at a cost. Operating within its confines means that you belong in several ways. You belong in language, in shared religion and in culture. It means you can hang on the corner, and that you'll be given "dap" (a fist bump) and welcomed wherever African Americans congregate. It means you always have a home. It's kind of like the old saying from the TV show *Cheers*—it's a place where everybody knows your name.

At least, this is how I suppose it must be. I don't honestly know. I've always been on the periphery of this experience, observing it, but not completely a part of it. I've always had a sense of the limits of the box, and I have resisted going within its limits for this reason.

Sometimes the black box means giving up too much in the name of being "cool' or "down." It can mean saying "no" to education and "yes" to stereotypical attitudes and ideas that ultimately lead nowhere. It can mean closed-mindedness to new ideas and diverse experiences. Sometimes it means adopting the attitude of only that which is "black" is worthwhile or good.

I'm not comfortable with feeling that, in order to maintain my authenticity as a Black American man, I must speak a certain way, choose certain pursuits and reject others. I can tell you with absolute certainty that I fully claim my blackness. How can I not, growing up where I grew up? If you were a brown-skinned boy in Baton Rouge in the 1960s, 70s and 80s, there was no mistake about your ethnicity. There were whites and there were blacks, and you clearly knew which one you were, no matter how light your skin.

If many Black Americans have invested in the black box and find in it a certain safety and community, some White Americans categorize blacks in their own black box that includes a similar raft of assumptions. For instance, if I'm black, then I must be a Democrat who likes fried chicken. I must like rap music and play basketball. The reality that I'm none of these things often results in a double-take from some, and my authenticity is questioned. Who said that I have to be any of these things?

Of course, there are other boxes for other communities. I speak of the black box, not because similar boxes don't exist for other communities, but because it's the one that, as an African American, I have the most knowledge of and because I know that African Americans place a different investment in it. Black Americans have invested more in the characteristics of their box, and this is both to our advantage and to our detriment.

Years after I first became aware of the black box, and my feelings like I was walking a tightrope above it, I wrote about some of these feelings in a blog post called "Black and White and a Target of Both" that was originally posted on the *CNN AC360* blog in 2008, then reposted in January of 2010. The subject was a young African American pilot, who was still in high school, named Brandon Henry who had been featured in a piece on *CNN*. When you understand that fewer than 2% of pilots are African American, you understand how far this young man had come, and how far he still has to go. Add to this another fact, provided by the U.S. Department of Justice, that young black men who are Brandon's age are more likely to go to prison than to college. Finally, factor in all the usual youthful stuff that side-tracks teenage boys of his age, including sex, experimentation with drugs and alcohol, cars and sports, and you get a picture of someone extraordinary.

As it turned out, Brandon Henry was from Louisiana, too. From the little he shared with me, in 2008 at least, not much had changed from my own experiences in the 1980s with rac-ism, colorism and trying to fit into the expectations and rules of a black world and a white world that thrives on limitations and negative stereotypes.

My own experiences tell me that this kid has probably got-ten teased mercilessly for his choices, for his interests, and for his determination. While there are several explanations for why there aren't more kids like Brandon, at least one of them is the power of the black box.

One of the examples of that power is how some professional blacks try to "walk the line" between how they behave around whites and other non-black people, and how they act in blacks-only environments. You know what I'm talking about. Around other blacks it's "say, bruh, whassup?" complete with dap, now called the fist bump, and a whole different way of holding the body. If a non-black enters the room, then the dialogue changes to "Hello, how are you today?"—just as stiff and formal as any Midwestern . . . well, news anchor.

I'm not saying that this sudden shift in speech and attitude is wrong, and I'm not saying that the shift is always affected, though I definitely think that sometimes it is. I've seen people "be black" when it's convenient, and reject it entirely when it's not so convenient. I've seen people take "staying black" to extreme levels.

None of that is who I am, and it never has been. I'm pretty much the same to everyone and there is no shifting in and out of black dialect or changing of manner from one context to the next. There is no need, in my mind, to define "black" in ways that change my goals or that affirm some of my goals and reject others. I'm like Brandon Henry. I had a dream from the time I was a really young kid that one day I could do what I'm doing now, and I've always worked toward it. If other people didn't believe it, and there were both whites and blacks who were only too happy to tell me that I'd never make it, well, that was their problem. It was never mine.

My relationships with white students at Baker High created a chasm between me and my fellow black students that left me walking a precarious tightrope. It was important to me that I be liked by others, just as it is for most teenagers. I liked my white friends, but I wanted to be liked by the black students, too. When I look back on it now, it seems as though I put myself through all kinds of emotional and social contortions just to seem "black enough," while not jeopardizing my friendships with kids who weren't black.

As uncomfortable and crazy as it was, it must have worked because both the white and black students voted for me to become President of the Senior Class. I was only the second black student to hold that office.

I was also voted "Most Liked Senior," or it may have been "Best Personality." I really don't remember. Funny, isn't it? The things you remember, and the things you don't.

I remember hearing that some of the white parents weren't pleased that a "nigger" was Senior Class President. Keep in mind that this wasn't long before there were streetlights or running water. This was 1983, but there I was, Senior Class President, whether they liked it or not.

I was also elected national president of all the Interact Club chapters across the country. The national recognition felt good. Still, I wouldn't call my high school experience the "Glory Days" like in the Bruce Springsteen song that was so popular that year. Not at all. For all it taught me, I wouldn't want to do high school again, not for any amount of money. The guys were sort of brutish, and the girls tended to be shallow and mean.

Rather, my glory days are every day that I'm alive. I'm always looking toward the future. The day I walked across the stage and accepted my diploma was, without a doubt, the beginning of the best days of my life. I was right, but it took me just a bit longer than I thought it would to figure out why.

CHAPTER 7

A Lesson on Faith

L ouisiana and I were soon to part company for a long, long time, and I was about to learn a powerful lesson about how other people's low expectations can have a powerful impact on your life—if you let them. Even more importantly, I learned that I had to have faith in myself, in my decisions and in my own beliefs about what I was capable of.

When I graduated from Baker High School and headed across town to Louisiana State University in the fall of 1984, I really didn't know what I wanted to do. Everyone thought I should work towards law school, like my father. I decided to study business, but I didn't care for it much. In fact, I hated it. I was working and studying for my degree and my progress was slowed by the fact that I just couldn't get excited by the course work. I dropped from taking several classes a semester to just a couple, then to one, then to taking "breaks" for entire semesters.

Around this time, I was "discovered" by a local department store and I started doing some modeling for their weekly advertisements. The extra money was great. Sometimes I earned several hundred dollars for an hour or less of work, but it just didn't seem like a "life plan." I was lost and I might have stayed that way if it hadn't been for two things—Jean West and the journalism program at LSU.

Unless you live in Baton Rouge or its surrounding suburbs, you probably don't know Jean West. At that time, she was the co-anchor of the evening news broadcast on WAFB, Channel 9. Currently, she is the sunrise anchor on WAVE, Channel 3 in Louisville, Kentucky. She was one of the first African Americans to hold this job. When I turned on the local news and saw an African American, a person who looked like me, in the news anchor chair, I remembered my childhood ambition. It suddenly seemed possible again, and when I learned that I could transfer out of the business program and into the journalism program, the die was cast. I made journalism my major, and reporting my career goal.

Admittedly, I struggled. I had a demanding work schedule, and I was putting myself through school with the money I earned from modeling and as a cashier at the local utility company, Gulf States. I worked as hard at LSU as I ever had at any point in my academic career. I wanted it that much. I had difficulty with the editing machines that pieced together the raw footage we shot with the student cameras in the broadcast lab. Editing was hard for me, not because I didn't have a sense of how the story should come together, but because I found the equipment difficult to master. Video editing still isn't my strongest skill, but in college I was still learning and having an extremely difficult time.

My professor was an older white man who had seemed dubious about me from the first day I walked into his classroom. There were several students that he was supportive of, but I wasn't one of them. He stopped me one day, after I'd failed to complete an editing project in the allotted time, and intoned in the hallway in earshot of anyone listening, "I don't know why you're here. You're not going to make it in this business."

Reading those words on the page, you might think this professor was simply delivering an opinion based on his professional judgment. You might think that, having seen hundreds of students in his classes, he had some idea of who would be able to succeed in the professional world and who would not. While many journalists, and others, have no doubt heard similar pronouncements, standing there that day, looking into his eyes, and feeling his condescending attitude, I knew with certainty what he was really telling me. He was saying, "There's no market for black journalists. Go find something more appropriate for your skin tone."

Criticizing my editing was the way he disguised or justified his beliefs, whether the accurate word for them is bias, prejudice or racism. It happens often. People don't want to express their racial prejudices, but they find ways (many times unconsciously) to express their feelings with other comments. If they believe blacks are inferior and they see a black person struggling with a particular task, it seems to validate their view. They don't have to say "you're inferior because you're black or Asian or Hispanic or a woman." Instead, they can say "This is too hard for you. Find something more appropriate to your strengths." When they see a white male struggling with the same task, however, the response is quite different. Instead of offering criticism, they may offer assistance, guidance or support. I've seen this happen time and time again in my career. Some people get resources, guidance, and assistance, and others don't. This still happens to me today. Sometimes the reasons aren't clear, and other times they are crystal clear.

This is an experience that isn't limited to immutable characteristics, like race or gender. Even white men face limitations in resources and support, sometimes over seemingly trivial differences and preferences that are often deeply unconscious. Affinities, categorizations and preferences are part of the rules of the game of life, and this isn't limited to journalism. This may be unfair, but it is a reality.

Even before my journalism professor told me to my face that I'd "never make it," I felt the subtle and the not-so subtle differences in the way I was treated and the way the white students were treated. I could see who was getting energy, guidance and attention and who wasn't. It's infuriating to be written off before you've even been taught what you need to learn. It's infuriating to be judged before you open your mouth, or before you've been given the opportunity to prove yourself as an individual. This is how some whites apply the black box to African Americans. They use a list of assumptions about what you can't do and where you'll end up if you happen to be black.

The impact of my professor's comment had a searing effect on me. I had a moment of clarity. I realized that if I stayed in Louisiana, my professor's words would probably come true. I realized that if I were going to "make it," I'd have to create a new opportunity for myself somewhere else. Perhaps, most importantly, I realized how much I wanted to make it, for myself and for all the other black students who, day in and day out, were told in ways both subtle and overt, that they weren't good enough.

That was my last semester at LSU. With $200 in my pocket, no connections, friends or even a serious plan, I moved to New York City. It was a crazy, bold, and youthfully reckless thing to do. New York City eats small town, Southern boys like me for breakfast, but I was determined to do whatever I had to do.

Don't tell me I can't do something, unless you want me to do it. Don't tell me "no." No is not an option. No is not an answer. I take "you can't" as a challenge. That professor started it, but the "no's" and the "you can'ts" are always around. I've heard them dozens of times since then, and each time it sounds an alarm in me that takes my career to the next level.

Once again, I have to quote the poem by children's author Shel Silverstein:

LISTEN TO THE MUSTN'TS

Listen to the MUSTN'TS, child
Listen to the DON'TS
Listen to the SHOULDN'TS
The IMPOSSIBLES, the WON'TS
Listen to the NEVER HAVES
Then listen close to me—
Anything can happen, child,
ANYTHING can be.

I've learned it by heart because it speaks so clearly to my life and the situations I've found myself in time and time again. Mr. Silverstein's verses became my guiding compass as I packed up my life and moved to New York City.

I landed in the Big Apple in November 1990, just in time to get a seasonal job in a department store, which lasted until the first days of the new year, January 1991. This was long enough for me to land a news trainee position at WNYW, Channel 5, the local FOX affiliate in New York City. The pay was a meager $5 an hour. Even in the 1990s, this wasn't nearly enough to live on in a city as expensive as New York.

I was broke, I didn't have a college degree, and I needed a second job to pay my rent. None of this mattered because I was on my way. I knew at that time that nothing else would stop me, and nothing has. I stepped out on faith, as the saying goes, and a way was made for me.

PART TWO:

You Don't Want to Fail on a Stage That Big

CHAPTER 8

A Lesson on Gratitude

When I look back at my decision to leave Baton Rouge, it astounds me. That single decision completely changed the course of my life. Along the way, I have been blessed by so many fortuitous meetings, circumstances and opportunities that it's almost overwhelming. In acknowledging and accepting those blessings, I learned some powerful lessons about hard work, kindness and gratitude.

Woodson

The Struggle for a College Degree

Most people think I just sailed through college after high school and have been in the news business for years.

They're wrong.

It took me almost *seven years* to get my college degree after I left LSU in the fall of 1990. Seven years, and every step of it was a struggle. Some might have given up on finishing school under the circumstances I experienced, and more than once I was encouraged to do just that—to *give up*. The LSU journalism professor's comments were a motivation that burned in me for many years. I couldn't quit. I wouldn't quit. I *would* get my degree. I *would* be a journalist. I would *not* accept his assessment of me or what I could accomplish in my life.

Still, it was tough. After months of part-time work, I had landed a full-time job as a new assistant for the FOX affiliate in New York City and worked my way up the ladder there for five years. Even at the station, there were people who told me that I didn't need a college degree, and that I was already on track to make a career with the experiences that I had and the work I was doing.

"It's only a piece of paper," they said. "You're doing fine without it."

It *was* only a piece of paper, but I never entirely believed that what it symbolized wasn't of value. After all, all of the news assistants, both white and black, working with me had undergraduate degrees from places like New York University and Columbia.

Whether it was "only a piece of paper" or not, it was a piece of paper I needed.

I paid for my education myself. This may sound surprising, given that I was indulged as a high school student and had a lot of family support. I discovered that college was something else altogether. I'd already spent years at LSU trying to figure myself out and choose a field of interest. By the time I moved to New York, I was a man. It wasn't right to ask my parents for any more help. It was up to me to make my way. Of course, I was broke, so there was no Columbia for me. The only realistic and afford-able choice I had, besides returning to Louisiana and LSU, was to attend CUNY, the City University of New York.

A friend of mine was finishing his Masters courses at Baruch College, one of CUNY's many schools, in Manhattan. He did some research for me and discovered that Brooklyn College, another of CUNY's schools, had a very respectable journalism program. In order to matriculate there, I would have to forfeit a number of my LSU credits and attend a CUNY community college for one semester. In essence, I would have to start over.

I made my decision on the spot. I took off a day of work and drove my beat up Jeep Wrangler to Kingsborough College in Sheepshead Bay in Queens and enrolled in community college to get the ball rolling. The only problem was that I had no idea how I would attend classes and work full time.

Whatever it took, I was determined to do it. I never really thought that I had much of my father's skill as a negotiator until I had to dig deep inside myself and find arguments to convince my co-workers to switch shifts so I could attend night classes at Kingsborough. I never thought of myself as having much physical endurance until, somehow, despite sleepless nights and impending exhaustion, I managed to complete that first trying semester.

I was never so glad to see an experience end! Surely the journalism program would be a bit easier. Ha!

After my semester at Kingsborough, I moved out of my apartment in Astoria Queens and into one in Brooklyn so I could be closer to Brooklyn College. My President Street apartment was about halfway between my job at FOX 5 and my new school. I hoped that the convenient location would save me time and make it easier for me to balance work and school. I was right and I was wrong. The location was great, but the balancing part never got easier.

I didn't sleep more than four straight hours each night for about a year. I did whatever it took to make it to my classes and complete the assignments. I would fall asleep on the subway and end up at the other end of the line, way out in the Bronx, in the wee hours of the morning and then have to get off, walk over to the opposite platform and take the next train back to Brooklyn. I barely had a social life. Everything was work and school, school and work.

I know many of you reading these words have had similar experiences; you know how tough it is to make the decision to return to school once you have adult responsibilities. Knowing how hard it was for me to do it with only *myself* to support and care for, I am truly amazed by those of you who have done it while taking care of your families.

If you've walked this road and tried to balance work and school, you know what it can do for your level of focus. Working full time while going to school gives those who attempt it a wonderful gift.

Since I had so little time, I developed the ability to see through the clutter at both work and school and boil every task down to the fewest possible steps needed. I learned how to prioritize my work. I learned how to get things done right the first time because I wasn't going to have time to do them again. At the time, I was grateful for those skills because I knew I'd never get everything I needed to get done without them. What I didn't realize then was just how valuable that efficiency, that "tell me what I need to know quickly and so I can remember it" attitude, would be in my future.

As it turned out, I was learning what most news viewers want from their newscasts. I didn't have a lot of time, so I began incorporating my valuable new skill into everything, including the stories I pitched and the stories I wrote for the anchors and reporters at my job. The results were amazing.

I excelled at work. I was still, technically, a production assistant, but my responsibilities increased. I became an assignment desk assistant, then a field producer, then a satellite feeds coordinator, and then I began to produce the cold opens to the newscasts. Finally, I became a writer for the *Ten O'clock News with John Roland and Cora Anne Mihalik*.

All of this, and I still didn't have a degree. I was still working on it, but it was slow going. I was doing so well that people still kept telling me, "You don't need it! It's just a piece of paper!"

Luckily for me, it was a time of transition in the FOX 5 newsroom. The station had just hired a feisty, young news director named Lisa Gregorisch. They say that when the student is ready, the teacher appears. In other words, some people just show up in your life right at the moment you need the kind of information, guidance or example they can provide. I believe in this, and I know that for me, Lisa was one of those people. Her guidance and direction really changed the way I thought about my career.

We hit it off right away, but it was after she'd been on the job a few weeks that she pulled me into her office for a serious chat.

"I like you. You're a hard worker and you're smart," she began, but I remember her next words exactly. "What do you want to be when you grow up?"

Of course, by that time, I was nearly 30, but life is a journey and we're always growing up, right? I told her everything about my life, about not having a college degree, and about wanting to keep my job at the station while working to get it. Regarding her question about what I wanted to be when I grew up, I answered truthfully, "an on-air personality."

"Show me your tape," she said.

By day's end, my tape was on her desk. It consisted of several of the projects I'd worked on in my journalism program, showing my abilities in front of the camera and behind it. She reviewed it. A few days later we had a frank conversation.

"Work on this and this and this," she told me, offering constructive criticism with an eye toward helping me achieve my goal of becoming an on-air personality.

That alone would have been significant assistance. Getting a one-on-one critique from someone in the profession is really helpful to a beginning journalist and I was very grateful. There's more. Lisa also promoted me from production assistant to full-time writer and assignment editor.

There is still more. She had crafted a game plan with the newsroom scheduler to allow me to attend my college classes more easily.

Lisa's mentorship proved to be invaluable to me. Later, as I neared the end of my studies, Lisa allowed me to report occasionally. It was Lisa who helped me find an agent to represent me as an anchor and reporter. Most newly-graduated journalists don't have agents at all, and especially not the caliber of agent she introduced me to. Most new journalists have to spend years toiling on-air in small markets before they get representation. Not me. To this day, I am represented by the agent Lisa introduced me to, Peter Goldberg of NS Bienstock, which is one of the most respected and powerful talent agencies in the world.

It's hard, even now, not to get emotional when I think about what Lisa did for me. She was my first mentor in the business. She is now the executive producer of the entertainment show *Extra*, and I don't make a move in this business without first having a conversation with my dear friend, Lisa Gregorisch-Dempsey.

When I think of the number of young people in our country right now who feel isolated and alone, I often think of how critically important it is for each of us to extend ourselves to offer support, advice and assistance. You don't have to be the same race or gender to provide that help and guidance—Lisa certainly came from a different background than I did. I believe she saw some qualities in me that reminded her of herself and she decided to help me make the most of them. That's what mentors do, and that's also why almost all of us have a role to play in helping young people overcome their perceived limitations.

School can be a place where young people find mentors, help and guidance (though certainly not always, as my own experiences at LSU proved). Brooklyn College proved to be as unlike my LSU experience as Manhattan is unlike Baton Rouge.

Unlike my LSU experience, the professors at Brooklyn College supported me and guided me. If they had any negative preconceptions about me and what I could accomplish, I never heard them. They were invaluable resources to me at that time and remain so to this day. They genuinely *helped* me. They *believed* in me. That help and support made all the difference, especially since I was now an older student, working full time, and struggling with adult responsibilities in addition to the pressure of school. My feelings about Brooklyn College are so strong and deep that I can truly say that the journalism program there picked up where St. Francis Xavier left off in terms of providing a creative outlet and a nurturing environment where I was able to develop my interests and abilities. I will refrain from waxing romantic about the smells and sounds of the place!

Instead, let me tell you about Adrian Meppen, an old cur-mudgeonly broadcast news professor, and Professor George Rodman, two men who would engage me in real conversations about their lives, their families and their experiences. They shared their wisdom about the business and this wisdom is really what made the difference for me. Young people sometimes *think* they are wise, but it's really not possible. Wisdom comes from time on this planet. Unlike skill, which can be achieved through repetition, wisdom is gained over time through experience.

By the time I left the company and the encouragement of these two men, not only did I feel like a better student and broadcaster, but also a better person. They knew the community and the city, and they sent us students out daily with our clunky VHS cameras to take it all in. We made stories out of it. Some of them were really bad stories, but for the most part, they were pretty good. Everything that I later did as a local reporter or an anchor, as a network correspondent, a documentarian, a main anchor on a cable network, and even now, as an author, was born in those early journalism assignments when my professors turned me loose, armed with little more than VHS camera and the city of New York.

Since I owe the faculty and staff a debt of gratitude too large to repay, I was positively humbled when I was invited to give the commencement address at the 2010 baccalaureate graduation ceremony at Brooklyn College. I was honored and excited, but my excitement quickly turned into fright.

Just like my initial reaction when I was asked to write a book, when I received the invitation to speak, I recall thinking, "Why on earth would any of these bright, young minds care about anything *I* have to say?"

Honestly, I considered calling Brooklyn College back and telling them "no." Since I'd already accepted the invitation, I couldn't bring myself to disappoint them.

Nonetheless, I found the invitation daunting. "Overwhelmed" is the most appropriate word to describe my emotions about giving that speech. My mind and heart were literally flooded with feelings and memories. I thought about everything I'd learned when I attended school there. I thought about the sacrifices I'd made to get my degree, and how much those sacrifices have been worth it. I remembered how it felt to miss my own graduation thirteen years earlier because I had just moved to Birmingham, Alabama to start my career as a full-time reporter and TV anchor. The strongest feeling was the feeling of gratitude. I've really had an amazing career, considering the fact that one professor told me I'd never make it.

Giving that commencement speech was surreal. I told the new graduates about my long journey from a struggling student, without enough money for a subway token some days, to my last visit to New York City on New Year's Eve that year. Far from worrying about subway fare, I'd actually gotten a police escort to join Anderson Cooper in Times Square that evening. Riding in that car and hearing police sirens, I'd looked out the window, wondering what was happening, the journalist in me sniffing for the story behind the wailing noise and the flashing lights. It took a moment to realize that *I* was the reason for the sirens. It was an overwhelming moment for me, realizing how far I'd come. It hadn't seemed possible that such a thing could be happening to me, Don Lemon. Inside, I hadn't changed. I still felt like that struggling student, but my circumstances had changed in ways I hardly could have imagined, and Brooklyn College is where it all began.

I cried like a baby through the whole speech.

Please understand, you have to have a thick skin to be in the news business. There's always criticism from editors, from producers, from viewers, and from critics. I don't let it bother me, and I tend to have such a high degree of focus that I don't remember much of what else is going on around me. I can't tell you how often I've had co-workers or friends say to me, "I hope you aren't upset about what I said the other day." My response is usually, "Why? What did you say?"

Quite honestly, if it's not within the scope of what I am working on, then I probably only give it a fraction of my attention. Ironically, the contradiction is that I'm actually a pretty sensitive guy. When something moves me emotionally, I allow it to. That commencement speech touched me to my heart's very core. I thought about my mother and my grandmother, my father and my stepfather, and about where I'd been and where I still hope to go. I was crying before I even got started. I just couldn't believe I was standing there—me, the one who wasn't supposed to make it. It all hit me at once. I realized how blessed I've been to do what I've dreamed of doing since I was little kid, annoying the whole household by imitating Peter Jennings in the living room of my mother's house.

It was an emotional day for me, and I didn't try to hide my feelings. I don't try to hide them when I'm working either. I don't think the viewers connect to someone who's robotic. They want someone to ask the questions they'd ask and relate to a story with the same emotions they feel. It's a lesson that I learned early in my career and it's one that I still use daily. I've been successful most of the time by simply being myself, following the stories that interest me, and asking the questions that pop into my mind. In fact, especially at CNN, I'm known for asking questions that some reporters and anchors might avoid. Brooklyn College gave me the formal training I needed that is now the cornerstone for most of my professional experiences.

As for that LSU journalism professor, the one who pronounced with certainty that I'd "never make it," when something wonderful or amazing happens to me, such as winning an Emmy or breaking some new ground in my career, it is entirely possible that he gets a news clipping in the mail.

Coming to Terms with Myself

College wasn't the only learning experience I undertook during my years in New York. I was also coming to terms with my sexual identity. Since I was knee high to a duck, I've known that I was gay, although it wasn't called that then. *Faggot, sissy, punk, funny*—those were the words people whispered in hushed tones when someone like me was around. Of course, sometimes they didn't whisper. They often yelled these words out at gay men, women and children, like weapons.

I had played the part of being straight in high school and even occasionally dated girls, but deep inside, I knew the truth. Even though I am sometimes attracted to women, I'm a gay man. While living in New York, this realization became stronger in my mind and I sought counseling to help me accept who I am and what it means for me, for my relationships and for my life.

To be completely honest, the need to come to terms with my sexuality was part of the reason I moved to New York City in the first place. I'm not sure how I would have managed to do it in Baton Rouge. New York's size and composition make it an accepting home for all kinds of people from all kinds of backgrounds. It was, and still is, a place where honest self expression is encouraged and expected. I felt free to explore my identity in New York in ways I don't think I ever would have in Louisiana. I felt free to seek out professional help to delve into my past in ways that I probably never would have done if I'd stayed in Baton Rouge. I felt free to drop my guard and experience myself outside the tight boxes of "home," "manhood," "culture" and "race" that bound me in the South.

While living in New York, I was finally able to come to grips with my childhood traumas of being sexually abused. I was able to talk it through and release it. I learned that molestation and sexual orientation had nothing to do with each other. Most predators are heterosexual and prey on children of the opposite sex, rather than same sex encounters. I was finally able to tell the people closest to me about what happened to me when I was a child and to shed tears with them over my inability to discuss the situation while it was happening. I was also able to "come out" in my daily life when I chose.

The fact is, I don't always choose to reveal my sexual orientation. Why should I? It's really no one's business. Please understand that, though it is something I often keep private, my sexual orientation is certainly *not* a secret. As the great American author James Baldwin wrote in his novel of racial, political and sexual tensions of the 1970s entitled *Another Country*:

The trouble with a secret life is that it is very frequently a secret from the person who lives it and not at all a secret for the people he encounters.[4]

I have lived with enough secrets to know how true these words are. The identity of my father was an "open secret," and even a grandmother I had never met before guessed it as soon as she saw my face. I lived with the secret of being molested, and while the people around me didn't know exactly what the trouble was, they knew I held myself apart from others in ways that left me isolated and unsure of myself much of the time.

---

4 *James Baldwin*, Another Country *(Vintage, 1992).*

In the end, secrets hurt me far more than they protected me. My "secrets" have fooled no one, and in the end did *me* more harm than good. This is exactly what James Baldwin, who himself was a black, gay American, was suggesting with his words.

I have absolutely no shame in being gay. It's a fact, much like the fact that my skin is brown, that I was born in Louisiana or that my favorite color is blue. It's a part of who I am.

I gave long and careful thought to including this revelation in this book. I talked it over with colleagues, mentors, family and friends. Many worried about this decision. After all, this is a risk. I know that there are many women who watch me on CNN who might be disappointed. I know that it may also have a negative impact on my career.

These concerns are valid. Almost every week, I get a letter, an email or have a conversation with an African American who tells me, "You're a role model for young black kids" or "I'm so glad you're there, on the news, doing what you do."

I am humbled each time I hear this, and I must say personally to all of you who watch me because you see me as a positive example of black manhood—nothing has changed.

Some of you may have different feelings about me after reading this book and I will have to accept that.

By revealing this information about myself I worry:

Will anyone want to watch me?
Will anyone still employ me?

What comes next?
I don't know.

After listening to my friends and family, my mentors and colleagues and consulting my own heart, I've decided that honesty on this issue is critical, perhaps *because* of the prejudices that still exist in the black community on the issue of homosexuality. It's important because of the difficulties black and gay young people face in coming to terms with their identities in a hostile world. It's important for *all* young gay people, including people like Rutgers University freshman Tyler Clementi, who might still be with us if not for the hatred and ignorance gay men and women face each and every day. It's important because the God that I believe in doesn't make mistakes, and He created each of us intentionally and for a purpose. So, on this subject, just as I have with so many other decisions and choices in my life, I'm choosing to "step out on faith" as the saying goes. What will be, will be. There are no accidents.

My time in New York helped me to embrace my identity. In those six years, I also learned the news business, earned my degree and prepared myself for the road ahead. By the time I left Brooklyn College in the spring of 1996, I was seasoned, confident and ready. I had said "yes" to critical truths about who I was and what I believed in. I could move forward.

I remain deeply grateful to so many people, including teachers, co-workers and friends, who helped me to hone my skills as a journalist during that time. I also thank them for their support as I came into a new level of knowledge and self-acceptance. Their kindness was, and continues to be, a lesson I will never forget.

CHAPTER 9

A Lesson on Persistence

T hrough hard work, faith, persistence and luck, my childhood dream came true.

It happened in ways I never would have expected, but nonetheless, it happened. The lesson I learned is that we should never,
ever give up on our childhood dreams.

Back to the South?

I needed a job, I needed an agent and now that I was finally
about to graduate, I needed a plan for my future. So what did

I do? I got on the elevator in a swank Times Square building with Christie Brinkley. Yes, Christie Brinkley, the former super-model.

I was on my way to my first meeting with Peter Goldberg, the man who would, with Lisa Gregorisch's introduction, become my agent. Just by chance, Ms. Brinkley boarded the same elevator. Starting with the doorman, moving on to the security guards, then to the couriers in the elevators with us and finally to me, she mesmerized every man in her presence. I couldn't worry about what on earth I would say to such a powerful man as Peter Goldberg; I was too busy staring at Ms. Brinkley, who is every bit as beautiful in person as she looks on magazine covers. When she exited a few floors before my stop in that Midtown office building, there wasn't any time left to worry about my meeting. Thinking about how gorgeous she is completely distracted me. I didn't have time to get nervous about meeting Peter!

As it turned out, I needn't have worried. Peter and I hit it off right away. We talked about my tape and then walked to a nearby deli for lunch. Not once did he pressure me to sign a contract before sending me back to the assignment desk on the Upper East Side at FOX Five.

Peter ended up becoming my agent and getting me my second job, but my first job came to me in a totally different way.

I owe it all to Rupert Murdoch.

I know. You're probably thinking, "Wow, Don Lemon was one really connected college student!"

Not exactly.

In the mid-1990s, Murdoch, who owns the FOX network, expanded the number of stations he owned by purchasing New World Television Group. Most of those stations had been ABC stations, but when Murdoch bought them, they became FOX stations overnight. Some of those stations' anchors and reporters felt that working for FOX was beneath them. They jumped ship to start ABC stations in their local markets. The mass exodus of the existing personnel created a talent vacuum at many of the new FOX stations.

It was a lucky break for someone like me, a newly-minted journalist with not much experience. WBRC FOX 6 News in Birmingham, Alabama needed a weekend anchor and reporter, and they wanted me.

Birmingham? To be honest, I wasn't crazy about returning to the South. I loved the freedom of New York City, the diversity, and the energy. I knew Birmingham would be slower, more racially black-and-white, and that social roles would be more constrained.

There was a part of me that didn't want to take the job. After all, I was working as a writer and an assignment editor for a New York station, which was a top market. I had a pretty good situation, but it wasn't ideal.

Much of my work in New York was behind the scenes and my dream was to be on the air. Birmingham offered me the opportunity of on-air reporting. It was a step closer to the career that I envisioned for myself. As reluctant as I was about returning to the South, I knew it was an opportunity I couldn't pass up.

Consequently, after spending six years in New York, I packed up the same broken down old Jeep that had brought me there and headed South. It was a 17 ½ hour drive, and I did it in a single day. I started work immediately.

For eleven consecutive months, every weekend I woke up at 4 am, anchored the morning news, went home and took a nap, went back to work around 2 pm and did the evening news. I also worked three days during the week as a reporter for the weekday newscasts. While the job wasn't awful, I must confess, I was constantly on the lookout for my next opportunity. Birmingham is a wonderful city and I met many great people there, but in many ways, being there reminded me of Baton Rouge, and not in a good way.

In spite of my best efforts, there were things I just hadn't been able to forget or completely forgive about being a black, gay man living in the South. My time in Birmingham let me know that I still had work to do on my feelings about race, identity and culture.

Don't misunderstand. It's not that there were any overt incidents of discrimination aimed at me. I felt subtly and often, the black box and its low and limited expectations being dropped over me in many situations. Instead of wanting to stay and fight it, the feeling made me want to run.

I continued to work hard, did my best at FOX 6 Birmingham, and kept looking for my next job elsewhere. Fortunately, the expanding FOX Broadcasting Network needed to fill more holes in their talent roster in even bigger markets. Peter negotiated the deal to get me out of Birmingham and on to St. Louis' KTVI as one of their prime time news reporters. I typically filed stories for the late newscast, as well. Occasionally, I filled in as the anchor of the morning and noon shows.

I signed a three-year contract, but I only worked in St. Louis for about a year and a half. It was at this time that NBC News came looking for me.

When the Network Calls, You Answer

I'd been in St. Louis for about a year when Peter called, asking for more videotape of my on-air work. He wanted to show it to Elena Nachmanoff and Pat Wallace from NBC.

I'd met Elena and Pat the year before at the National Association of Black Journalists (NABJ) Convention in Chicago. Elena was the head of Talent Development for NBC News, and Pat Wallace was the head of the NBC-Owned and Operated Stations News Group. I was still under contract with FOX when I met them and couldn't talk with them about opportunities with NBC. In the months since our meeting, a window in my contract opened, allowing me to explore other opportunities.

I put together a new tape and sent it to Peter. As soon as I got the call that Elena and Pat wanted to talk, I was off to New York to visit 30 Rockefeller Plaza, the home of NBC News.

I was excited to be going back to New York, even if only for a short visit. Mostly, I was excited by the prospect of working for NBC. There's a certain prestige that comes with working as a correspondent for a network, as it's an entirely different world from working as a reporter for a local station. I imagined myself hanging out with Katie Couric, Tom Brokaw, the late David Bloom and other NBC journalists whose work I admired. Picturing myself working alongside them, and only three years out of college, was like stepping into a beautiful dream, for it really did seem like a dream. It didn't seem like this could ever possibly happen, regardless of the number of meetings I had.

I flew from St. Louis to New York, feeling like Cinderella on the way to the ball, knowing well that at midnight my coach would turn right back into a pumpkin.

Elena and Pat liked my tape.

"We've heard really good things about you," they said. "We think with a bit more time and experience you'll be exactly what we need at NBC. So we want you to meet with Steve Schwaid, the news director of the NBC affiliate in Philadelphia. If he likes you and wants to hire you, and if you do well there, we want to bring you on as a network correspondent in a few years time."

I didn't believe them.

Seriously.

I thought they were kidding me. Yanking my chain.

They weren't. They set the appointment for me to interview with Steve Schwaid the very next day. Within a few hours, I was on an Amtrak train from New York to Philly, instead of on a flight back to St. Louis.

Philadelphia's WCAU was, and still is, located in a big gymnasium of a building just outside the city limits. Oddly, even though the city is large, one of the station's main competitors, the ABC station, was, and still is, located directly across the street within rock-throwing distance. As far as I know, no one ever threw any *actual* rocks at the competition, but during Steve Schwaid's tenure at WCAU, a lot of *figurative* rocks were thrown by both stations as they jockeyed for ratings in Philadelphia's competitive news market.

Steve Schwaid isn't a physically imposing guy. He's probably about 5'10", but his personality is gigantic—so huge it seems amazing that his body can contain it. In the hubbub of a newsroom the size of a football field, Steve's voice could be heard above everything, barking questions, instructing reporters, anchors and producers, and talking to the TV monitors as he watched the competition. I sat and observed for a bit before getting the go ahead to enter his office, taking it all in and trying to imagine myself working there. It reminded me of what it had been like to work for the local affiliate in New York.

Suddenly, blue flashing lights went off all around the station. I'd never seen anything like it and it must have shown on my face because Steve's assistant glanced at me and said, "Uh oh, breaking news." One second later, Steve himself zoomed by me, making a beeline line for the assignment desk. I don't exactly remember what the breaking news was, but I do remember that the station's chopper was deployed, along with two reporters and two live trucks. Within minutes, they were reporting live from the scene, first from the chopper, then from the reporters on the ground.

I later learned that Steve had installed the blue flashing lights as a "call to arms" for his news team. Whenever the lights flashed, which they did every time there was breaking news, everyone who could see those lights was to report to the newsroom to see if they could assist.

Eventually, things calmed down enough in the newsroom for Steve to talk with me. He liked me.

As soon as I was able to negotiate a release from my obligations to St. Louis, I joined WCAU in Philadelphia and I was in training to eventually become a correspondent with NBC News.

This Blue Light is NOT the K-Mart Special

Sure enough, on my first day on the job, Steve's flashing lights called me into action and I was off to report on a big FBI gun bust in northeast Philadelphia. To this day, I have that 'all hands on deck' philosophy when it comes to breaking news. Without hesitation, even if I'm not at work, I call in and ask if I can be of assistance. This philosophy has put me out front on many big stories, including plane crashes, explosions, tornadoes, hurricanes, floods and even the 9-11 terrorist attacks.

While I certainly have always had ambitions and hopes for what I wanted to accomplish in my career, at the end of the day, individuals are far less important than making sure that the story is told. When important news is breaking, it's crucial to be able to put ego aside and do whatever needs to be done to make sure the viewers get the information they want and need.

I was happy to be in Philadelphia. New York was just a few hours away and I felt like my career was moving in a direction that I was pleased with, even if I wasn't quite saying "hello" to Katie Couric on the elevators at 30 Rock.

The Today Show

I was sitting in a news van outside of Philadelphia City Hall, getting ready to do a live broadcast when I got the call.

"Can you come up to New York and do the news breaks for tomorrow morning's *Weekend Today* show?"

The Today Show, as you know, is NBC News' extremely popular morning show. At that time, the weekday show was hosted by Katie Couric and Matt Lauer, and the weekend program was hosted by Soledad O'Brien and the late David Bloom. This was a *big* deal for me—a very, very big deal.

I stammered out a "yes," listened to the details of what I supposed to do and where I was supposed to be and hung up. It was really hard to stay focused on the story I was covering after getting a call like that!

Later, at the post-show meeting after the newscast, the news director made the announcement, "Well, our own Don Lemon will be doing the news breaks on *Today* this weekend!"

I remember there was some polite applause, but I definitely had the feeling that there was a little jealousy in the room. Most journalists are competitive people, and competition is part of what keeps everyone working hard to do their best work. I'm sure there were people in the room who were thinking things like:

"Why him?"

"He hasn't even been here that long!"

There might have even been someone who was thinking, "He's some kind of affirmative action pick."

I don't know that for sure, but it wouldn't surprise me at all if someone had that thought.

No one said anything that wasn't congratulatory to me. Even if they had, it wouldn't have mattered to me. I was too excited and too focused on this big, new opportunity to let anyone's jealousy bring me down.

That evening, I called my mom.

"Be sure to watch the *Today* show this weekend," I told her. "One of my stories is airing."

I didn't tell her I was going to be reading the news updates. I wanted her to be surprised. I was dying to tell her, but the bigger payoff would be to let her see me there on her television. It would be so exciting for her to hear Soledad and David saying, "And here's Don Lemon with this morning's news."

I knew she would be thrilled and excited to see me on *The Today Show*. I was pretty excited myself. This was the "big time." This was the dream. If you can imagine yourself having the chance to become a part of your favorite program, you can begin to understand what that moment meant to me. It was almost surreal.

After the late newscast Friday night at WCAU, I took the Amtrak train from Philly to New York. I hardly slept a wink that night and was up long before they called for me at 4 am. A black sedan was waiting for me just outside the hotel, even though I could have easily walked the short distance between the hotel and 30 Rock. Then again, who would want to walk anywhere at that hour of the morning?

Security and staff were expecting me. I was led first to a dressing room, where the staff grabbed my suit, shirt and tie to steam them to perfection for the television cameras. I sat there in my boxer shorts, T-shirt and black dress socks, waiting, and drinking what felt like a gallon of coffee to try to keep myself alert. I could hear Soledad and David talking in the halls.

Once my wardrobe had been tidied up and I had dressed, they led me to Makeup. The girls in the make-up room made small talk and tried to make me comfortable, but my nerves were out of control, enhanced, no doubt, by the over-consumption of caffeine. Then they led me out to the set to meet Soledad and David and the weatherperson, Janice Huff. Janice and I became instant friends, and we still are. The floor director gave me a quick rehearsal on cues and camera positions, then the lights came on, the music came up in my ear piece and we were on the air.

I can't tell you what this felt like for a kid who used to entertain his family at night by imitating national television anchors to be sitting in that chair. It took every ounce of concentration I had not to cry when I heard the *Today* show theme in my earpiece. I imagined my mother, sitting in front of her TV, watching her son broadcasting all over the country on the most successful morning television show of all time.

Today airs an hour later in Baton Rouge, central time, and the minute my first news break came on in my family's time zone, my cell phone started buzzing and buzzing. It didn't stop all day. They were so proud of me, and my heart was full. I had achieved something I'd dreamed about since I was a little kid.

Over the next couple of years, while I was still employed full time in Philadelphia, I was asked to do the news breaks frequently for *Today.* While every time was a thrill, nothing could ever compare to that very first time.

To my great surprise, a short time later, CNN approached me with a job opportunity. I was completely blown away. I had only been on-air for five years, but I had *two* national news networks, NBC and CNN, interested in me at the same time.

CNN or NBC?

After earning my chops at their NBC affiliate in Philadelphia, the number three news market in the nation, NBC was ready to take me to the network. This meant moving back to New York, where I'd be submitting news reports for all of their broadcasts, including *The Today Show* and *The NBC Nightly News.* I liked the idea, but I was seriously considering CNN.

This was 2001. For most of the prior two decades, CNN had been unmatched as the provider of 24-hour news, but in the mid-90s, it found itself competing with MSNBC and FOX

News. Even with this competition, CNN was still a very powerful and pervasive network and the home of several journalists
whose work I had long admired, including Bernard Shaw. Its
coverage of crises throughout the 1980s and 1990s (the Chal-
lenger Disaster, the Gulf War, President Clinton's sex scandal
and trial, just to name a few) had made it one of the most
respected and well-known news organizations around. People
in power still talk about the "CNN effect" or the impact that a
story or issue gathers when the nation begins to follow it on a
continuous news cycle.

The possibility of joining CNN instead of NBC was an attractive one.

I saw the potential for a real opportunity with the network,
and I was excited by it. There was also a question of loyalty, however. NBC had invested so much in my talent. Gratitude made
me hesitate, but something else cemented my decision.

I got a call from a manager at CNN, who no longer works
there, who told me to reject NBC and join CNN because, "You
don't want to fail on a stage as big as *NBC Nightly News*." I know
he meant the comment with the best of intentions, even as a
selling point and advantage to starting with CNN instead of
NBC, but it was the wrong bait. It implied that I couldn't make
it at NBC. There were shades of that LSU professor all over
again in the words.

NBC, however, had the right hook for my personality. They
said, "We think you can do it. And we're going to give you the
support you need to make you successful here."

I said "no" to CNN in 2001 and "yes" to NBC. Of course, CNN and I were hardly through with each other, but as we say in news, "more on that later!"

CHAPTER 10

A Lesson on Facing Fear

As a general assignment correspondent for NBC News, I sometimes found myself in frightening situations, facing death and destruction, disease and the awesome power of Mother Nature. Though I was scared, the experiences encouraged me to push further and to stretch my perceptions to their utmost. It helped that I loved my job. I loved the adrenaline rush of covering a good story well, no matter how dangerous. This is the lesson I learned—that feeling like you're doing something worthwhile and important, something in the service of others, is the best medicine for defeating fear.

The Aftermath of 9–11

I was in Philadelphia on September 11, 2001. In a few weeks, I would join NBC News, but I hadn't left yet.

Still, New York City is only an hour away from Philadelphia by Amtrak train and I reported on the tragedy for my Philadelphia viewers while frantically trying to get in touch with many of my friends who commuted from Philly to New York every day.

There's not much I can say about 9-11 that hasn't already been said. Beyond the planes and buildings, what has stayed with me the most are the looks on the survivors', faces as they fled the dust clouds that enveloped the city streets as the World Trade Center buildings toppled. Not a day goes by that I don't think about the horror of it all, how it changed the world and how jumpy it made all of us. Just two months later, everyone thought another attack had happened.

On November 12, 2001, as a brand new correspondent for NBC News, I found myself reporting from the crash scene of American Airlines Flight 587 in Rockaway, Queens. The plane when down shortly after it took off from New York's JFK airport, killing all 260 people aboard and five more on the ground.

In the early hours after the crash, everyone thought it was another terrorist attack. Ultimately, the National Transportation Safety Board eliminated terrorism as a cause, but in the beginning, the crash of Flight 587 fueled the nation's angst.

As one of the correspondents on the scene, I witnessed the zombie-like looks on the faces of people who escaped when the jet engines, nose gear and wreckage plummeted toward the earth as the plane plunged down onto their homes. The expressions of survivors are something that I'll never get used to no matter how many times I see them. Their expressions resonate because they are reminders of how fragile and random life can seem. A plane falls from the sky and kills your next door neighbor, but not you. Why? Luck? Fate? Divine intervention? We don't know. This combination of relief and guilt is something I've seen in the faces of many disaster survivors and it's unforgettable.

My other memory is of the first-responders. Many of the same still-exhausted rescuers who had run into the burning World Trade Center buildings leapt right back into action in Queens just a few weeks and miles from where those towers once stood. Their dedication and courage in the face of such grim tasks remain an inspiration to me.

It seemed like the bad news was unrelenting and everyone's anxiety, including mine, was particularly high. Less than a year after joining NBC News as a correspondent, I found myself in a situation that tested my own courage and commitment.

Covering the DC Snipers

They were shooting people as they walked along city sidewalks, as they returned to their cars after shopping or as they pumped gas at neighborhood gas stations and no one knew where they would strike next. The DC Snipers were terrorizing Washington, DC and the surrounding suburbs, reminding a nation already on edge that no one was safe.

I was the lucky one from NBC News dispatched to DC. I can't tell you how I felt pulling off the DC beltway into a neighborhood on the outskirts of the city, and noticing how quiet and empty the streets were. Even worse was the realization that hit me just a moment later—I needed to stop for gas.

By this time, several of the snipers' victims had been killed at gas stations, while pumping gas. I already knew that each had been killed by a high-powered rifle, fired at a distance. You'd never know you were in danger and that a shot would be fired at you like that. You'd never know you were in the sights of the shooter at all.

It was a chilling thought, but my gas needle was nearly on "E." I had to fill the tank. I pulled into the nearest gas station and sat there in my car. The place was deserted. It was so quiet, and there were hardly any cars on the roads and hardly any people out and about. I didn't want to get out.

I sat there, imagining a sniper lining me up in the crosshairs of his weapon as I sat in my car debating with myself, "Get out? Stay in?" As soon as I opened my car door and stood up, he would have a clear shot. I sat. I contemplated my gas gauge, calculating whether there was enough left to get to the hotel. Even then, I would have to get out of the car. Both at the pump, and later at the hotel, I would, however briefly, be exposed.

I continued to sit there, contemplating the dark streets, and trying to "see" the unseen. It was the gas gauge itself that finally put my body in motion. It was just too close to "empty" to chance driving much further, especially on unfamiliar roads. I slowly opened the car door, sheltering as much of my body as I could, as I began my transaction. Picture me—crouching behind the gas pump, and wedging myself against my car door. All the while, I kept glancing around furtively, just in case.

It was the fastest gas I've ever pumped. Since then in my career, I've been to more harrowing places and done scarier things. I have to admit that pulling into that deserted gas station outside of the District of Columbia that night, knowing that already three people had been killed while pumping gas, and three others murdered while doing equally mundane activities, I was as scared as I've ever been.

The very next morning, news came of another shooting, of a man pumping gas at a Sunoco station in the Virginia suburbs, and all my fears seemed completely justified. Before it was over, ten people would die in those three awful weeks.

Everyone believed at the time that the sniper or snipers were either domestic terrorists or some single-minded crackpot with a grudge, like Timothy McVeigh, the bomber responsible for the loss of hundreds of lives at the Alfred P. Murrah Building in Oklahoma City back in 1995. All the experts had warned of a white man or white men in a white van. When the DC snipers were ultimately caught and it was revealed that they were a pair of black men, I was as surprised as anyone else. When I learned, however, that one of the two, John Allen Muhammed, had purchased their car of terror in Camden and had family in the Philadelphia area, I didn't hesitate to use my knowledge of the area to try to get a more intimate look at the men behind such a deadly shooting spree.

I decided to call Mr. Muhammed's Philadelphia family members and ask them if they wanted to share what they knew about the man who had been charged with ten counts of murder and who seemed to be the diabolical mastermind of an internal "jihad" against every day Americans.

Many of my colleagues laughed. They were sure my interview request would be denied, flat out.

After all, many of the relatives of the sniper pair were so ashamed and angry that they were avoiding any conversations with the press, and their feelings were completely understandable. I would have respected that answer from these family members if that had been their response, but I had to at least ask.

I asked.

I asked carefully and politely, speaking to them as a fellow African American who hoped to bring full life to their feelings and their story. I wanted them to know that I understood that, while John Allen Muhammed had committed these terrible crimes, I appreciated that they, his family, were blameless. I wanted them to feel safe in talking with me about what they knew, what they could understand about the things that might have led up to Mr. Muhammed's actions and where they felt things had gone so horribly, terribly wrong in this man's mind.

They didn't say "no." They talked to me. In fact, I was the only reporter they spoke with, which was a real *coup* for me at a time when everyone wanted to know about these men and what made them tick.

When I learned that John Allen Muhammed had been born

John Allen Williams in Baton Rouge, Louisiana in 1960, six years before I was born, I had the feeling of someone walking over my own grave. Same city, same basic time period, and such different fates.

We learned more about him in the months and years that followed, like his strange military career where he became a crack shot but had problems with his superior officers; his conversion to the Nation of Islam; his abusiveness to his wives; the children he abandoned; the allegations of fraud that drove him from the Caribbean isle of Antigua and his unlikely friendship with the young Lee Boyd Malvo.

He remained unrepentant for his crimes until his execution in 2009 and, I'm certain, much of what really drove this man died with him.

I still think of that story sometimes, on a dark and quiet night, when I get out of my car to pump gas, and I wonder how two people, me and John Allen Muhammed, can be in the same city at the same time and have such radically different lives.

But for the grace of God, the love of my family and the drive to bring my childhood dreams to life, there go I. It's something to think about.

Chills and Thrills

It's funny, but sometimes covering one story ends up making me think about something else altogether.

For example, while covering the Space Shuttle Columbia's

explosion outside of Houston, Texas in February 2003, I found my mental wheels turning on a very different story. James Byrd was on my mind.

If that name doesn't automatically ring a bell, his story will. He's the black man who was dragged to death behind a pickup truck on a dark country road by a few good ol' boys who thought killing a nigger would be a good time. Not in the 1920s or 1930s, when lynchings and killings were a part of the strange fruit landscape of the Jim Crow South, but in 1998.

We like to think that this stuff doesn't happen in America anymore, but the sad reality is, for all the progress we've made, we still have people whose hatred leads them to shocking and disgusting acts of cruelty and violence. The James Byrd case is an example.

After having his ankles wrapped in heavy logging chain, Byrd was dragged behind a pick-up truck for two miles over rough pavement. Unconscious for most of it, he was killed when his body hit a culvert and his right arm and head were severed from his body. His torso was eventually dumped in front of the black cemetery in Jasper, Texas.

While covering the Columbia disaster, I wondered if I might have time to visit the infamous road where Mr. Byrd met such an ugly and painful end, and perhaps do some kind of follow-up story, on my own. Not because the network asked me to, but because a crime that horrific deserves remembrance. I hoped that, perhaps, if I filed it, the network might use it.

I never got the chance to file the story, but I did get the chance to visit the road and the culvert where Byrd's headless body came to rest. I shivered just looking at it.

I interviewed a guy who found a chunk of the Columbia space shuttle on his property. I thought of the seven brave astronauts who died in the explosion, but my mind kept returning to an image created by my own imagination—the image of James Byrd's mangled, headless body lying lifeless on a dark Texas road.

Imagination is a trait I've always known I had. While working as a general assignment correspondent with NBC News, I discovered another trait that I hadn't been aware of before.

I'm a thrill-seeker!

Perhaps you are not surprised, but I was. I discovered it chasing hurricanes.

Although hurricanes can have different paths, do different levels of damage and wreak different degrees of havoc, they can also be awfully similar. As the reporter covering them, you can depend on two rules:

Number one: You are going to get wet.
Number two: You are going to be blown around by the wind.

If you want to add a third rule to hurricane coverage, it would be this:

The reporter who is willing to get the wettest and blown around the most, will get the most dramatic images. This is how I discovered that I'm a thrill seeker, because I was willing to get really wet, and really blown around, to the point that my camera guys were scared to death, both for me and for themselves.

Covering hurricanes for the 2002 and 2003 seasons, we got some great footage of the storm surge slamming over flood walls in Louisiana, Florida and Texas. I got really wet and the wind was so fierce I felt like my body was bent parallel to the ground. During those two seasons, I'd venture out on boats into flood waters, trying to get the best images. I always wore a life vest, a habit that carried with it the memory of my dad's unfortunate brush with drowning. The camera crew would tie a rope around me. If I got too adventurous, they would pull me to safety. Instinctively, we'd know when enough was enough, they'd pull me back and we would retreat to shelter.

Over and over, the crew would say to me:

"After this we gotta go in, Don. We gotta get to shelter."
I wasn't having it.
"OK, one more stand up," I kept saying. "Just one more."
The truth was, I was having fun.
Crazy?
Probably. But I have to tell you, hurricane reporting is a *rush!*
For me, it's the same thrill some guys get from bungee jumping or from extreme cycling or race-car driving. It's terrifying to watch, but when you're the guy in the middle of it, you are definitely afraid. At the same time, you're compelled to push yourself to the absolute limit.

Or at least that's how I felt then.

The hurricane that changed my life and so many others came years later. You know all about her—she's a hurricane named Katrina. Since Katrina, I feel differently about hurricanes, but not about pushing myself. I still love a thrill!

"Hey—you're that guy from TV. Do you know...?"

If I ever start to get a big head, or let my ego run away with me, there's nothing like working for a big network like NBC (or CNN!) to keep you humble.

Plenty of days, I've been walking the street somewhere, feeling pretty good about the story I covered the night before or some nice comment I've gotten about my work, when someone would approach me and say:

"Hey. I know you. You're that guy. You're on TV."

This is usually the place where I smile self-deprecatingly and say, "Yes, I'm Don Lemon."

My name is usually met with a blank stare.

"Yeah, I've seen you. Do you know Katie Couric?"

"Yes."

"Wow . . . would you tell her that (insert name here) said 'hi' and that I watch her every morning (this was back when Katie was still doing *The Today Show*.) Tell her I just love her."

Occasionally, I've had the same conversation, only the passerby wants me to send greetings to Matt Lauer, or Tom Brokaw or Brian Williams.

It's the sort thing that reminds me of my sisters and their loving, earthbound efforts to keep my big head from floating me right off to Mars!

"Don thinks he's Big Time," I can hear them saying when I get a little full of myself or when I start thinking that I've done a really good job with something. "Oh Lord! That head's gonna take over the world!"

People on the street offer me the same earth-tethering reality, and I'm grateful for it. Sure, I do a good job, but I'm no Katie Couric.

A Change of Pace

I really wasn't looking to leave NBC when the opportunity came. The writing, producing and reporting discipline I learned at the network is invaluable. My career path might have been very different without learning to succeed on that "big stage." I might have languished for decades in Birmingham or St. Louis. Both are respectable markets with very talented journalists working in them, but had I stayed at either place, I might never have experienced some of the things I did. By working at NBC News, I had earned national respect. I didn't fail there. In fact, I was doing well.

I was also well aware that general assignment reporting, even if it was for a major news network, wasn't exactly the goal I set for myself when I was practicing my anchorman voice in my grandmother's living room. I always kept my eye on that first dream, and I was beginning to feel like it might be time to make another move.

Sometimes, it's hard to give up something good and take a chance on something better, and I'll be honest, deciding to leave NBC News was a tough decision for me for many reasons, not the least of which was the power and respect that come with working for an organization as well known as NBC.

PART THREE

Chicago

CHAPTER 11

A Lesson in Happiness

I was a correspondent for a national network. I was covering important stories. I had proved myself on the "big stage" and earned the respect of my colleagues. But I wasn't happy.

I kept hearing myself as a child in my family's living room, doing my anchorman routine. Anchoring was what I really wanted to do, and I knew it. I had such a sweet gig, the kind most journalists would do anything to get! Could I really just walk away from it?

I didn't know, but soon, I got the chance to find out.

In the spring of 2003, when I had been with NBC News for just under a year, Peter, my agent, called.

"You've got an offer here. Any interest in becoming one of the lead anchors for NBC's Chicago affiliate?"

He gave me the full back story of WMAQ Chicago's problem. One anchor was seriously ill with cancer and his health issues meant he wouldn't be able to continue much longer. Their weekend anchor wasn't available, and yet another contender had been lured away by another station. WMAQ needed to re-stock their bench, to borrow a sports metaphor, and they wanted to know if I would take the 5 pm anchor position.

Hmmm.

Here was an anchor position in a large city with lots of possibilities for me. On the other hand, I had this plum network gig that most journalists would kill for.

I thought about it, but in the end, responded with an emphatic, but polite, "No, thank you." I just couldn't walk away from NBC and all that it represented.

What's "Happy" Got to Do With It?

A few months later, I ran into Steve Schwaid in the halls of 30 Rock. He was no longer the news director in Philadelphia. He had moved up to become chief of NBC Owned and Operated Stations News Group. There was no doubt he knew about my Chicago offer when he looked me straight in the eyes and asked, "Are you happy, Don?"

Faced with such a direct question from a man whose judgment I'd grown to respect, I searched myself for an honest answer.

The truth was, I wasn't that happy. I felt like I *should* be happy. I was working for NBC News for goodness sakes! The reality is that increasingly, I found myself discontent.

Why?

Well, the first reason was because I had no life.

I spent more time on the road than in my apartment. My friends from Philadelphia were in my apartment more than I was! Once, when I came back from a long stint on the road, I saw a friend in front of my apartment building. He had come to New York for the weekend, and was borrowing the place, with my permission, of course. Unaware of me right behind him, he walked into the building, greeted the doorman and headed to the elevators. As I grabbed my bags and followed him inside, my own doorman stopped me.

"Who are you visiting, sir?"

"I live here," I told him, giving him my apartment number.

"Really? May I see your driver's license?"

The guy actually took my license, went back to the office and checked my identification against the lease on file.

Wow. He knew my *guests* better than he knew me. That's how little time I spent at home.

The second reason was my exhausting schedule.

Here's an example of how crazy my life was:

Remember the SARS scare in the Spring 2003? SARS was an upper respiratory disease that was spreading quickly and at that time no one knew what caused it or how to cure it. I was shipped off to Canada to report on the rising numbers of cases of the disease, with literally only the clothes on my back. I was *supposed* to be gone for just a day. I was *supposed* to fly up, do the story and come right back. That's what was *supposed* to happen.

I left the *Weekend Today* set, headed to the airport, and didn't return for weeks. The simple story I set out to cover developed into something much more complex, and I was asked to stay in Canada as more cases of the disease were reported and to follow the developing outbreak. I had to buy clothes, underwear, toiletries—everything. So much for a "one day" assignment.

It was also a dangerous assignment. So little was known about SARS (severe acute respiratory syndrome) that the camera crews and producers were afraid to come anywhere near anyone who showed symptoms of the illness. The disease was that serious and that infectious. I remember doing a story on a man who had developed the symptoms. He agreed to do an interview with us, but the logistics were complicated because no one wanted to get anywhere near him. The sound technician dropped the microphone in the man's front yard. His wife came outside, picked it up and secured it to her husband's lapel inside the house. He sat in the window while I interviewed him from the sidewalk. While I wasn't afraid of being close to the man, I had to respect that my camera crew was uncomfortable. They had children and wives and husbands and were justifiably afraid of taking the disease home to them. If I had gotten too close to the man, they probably wouldn't have wanted to work with me anymore.

I can't tell you how embarrassed I was when the crew unplugged the microphone from the camera and left it and the cord on the couple's front lawn. They didn't want to touch it for fear of becoming infected. This is what we had to do to get that man's story told and to give voice to what people who had SARS were dealing with in countries world-wide.

As far as I know, the man survived, thank God, but SARS killed almost 800 people around the world and infected ten times as many before a cure was found. It was a scary and dangerous time.

The third reason I wasn't happy was more professional and somewhat surprising. The truth was, I wasn't really feeling challenged by my work as a correspondent at NBC News.

In the early months of 2003, right up until I did the SARS story, my only assignment had been covering the protests of Americans who opposed President Bush's decision to declare war on Iraq. I spent months in satellite trucks in Times Square, at the United Nations and other locations around Manhattan, watching protests and in readiness in the case of another terrorist attack in retaliation for the escalating war. I became very familiar with NBC's makeshift studio perched just above the General Assembly Hall of the United Nations. I did many of my MSNBC live shots from there.

All the attention was on the run up toward war. The action was in the war zone and in Washington. I was not in either of those places. I was the low man on the totem pole and was not getting much airtime. There was little interest in the stories I pitched state-side, even if they were war-related.

So, though it might sound strange, by the time the SARS story started to percolate to the top of the news, it was, in an odd way, a welcome relief because at least it was something different. I just hadn't expected to be away for so long.

So here I was, in what I thought was a dream job, and unhappy. I was never home. I didn't have a life. I never saw my friends anymore. Even my own door man didn't know who I was. I wasn't even getting to do the kinds of stories I wanted to do. Was this really what I wanted?

Everyone has those moments in life where you get what you thought you wanted and then realize that maybe it wasn't what you wanted after all. That was me. By the time Steve Schwaid asked me, "Are you happy?" I was sitting at that moment, wrestling with what to do about it and completely unsure of what direction to take next.

It was still possible to at least *talk* to the people in Chicago.

By the time I left Canada, I was ready to go to Chicago and do just that.

Signs and Omens

It was hard enough for me to decide to do that much, but things got murkier. I'm not particularly superstitious, but when bad weather diverted my plane from Chicago to St. Louis and I had to spend the night there, I got nervous. Only a few short years before, I had lived and worked in St. Louis.

Was it a sign?

Was someone or something trying to tell me something?

Would taking the job in Chicago mean "going backwards?"

Hmm.

I don't know if it was a sign or not. It's not impossible. I know you've heard the stories of people who just get a feeling that they shouldn't get on the plane, and they listen and refuse to board. Then the plane crashes. Or those who narrowly avoided being on the scene of a disaster because of a flat tire or forgotten keys. Sitting in a hotel in St. Louis because my plane was grounded by a snowstorm had me wondering if I was leaping from the frying pan straight into the fire.

Maybe I was supposed to turn around and go back to New York?

In the end, I went to Chicago, met with WMAQ's management and told them "no."

I was spooked.

I worried that it would, indeed, be a step backward. After all, hadn't I dreamed my whole life of having an on-air job with a national network? Isn't that exactly what I had?

Having achieved the mythical "network" job, why would I return to a local station, no matter how large the market, no matter how much they offered in terms of control of my stories and my time?

So, I said "no."

Then, just like that, I was back in my little satellite truck in Times Square, killing time, watching protests.

Oh boy.

Immediately, I wondered if I'd made a huge mistake. Was this one of those "no's" that was based on what I so despised—fear, doubt and self-protection?

When Larry Wert, the then-general manager of WMAQ called to ask me to reconsider, I was willing to listen.

"I promise, I'll make this move worth your while," he said. "And if it doesn't work out, we'll get you back to the network. Come back out and talk to us again, Don."

I thought to myself, why not? Chicago certainly didn't hurt Oprah Winfrey! Maybe it would be good for me, too.

I flew to Chicago again, and this time there was no snowstorm. I went to dinner with retiring anchor, Warner Saunders and talked about the possibilities. This time I accepted the job.

Maybe that snowstorm had been trying to tell me something after all. The excitement began immediately.

Welcome to WMAQ

My first day at WMAQ, I was supposed to take care of some paperwork and meet the staff, learn the office, and things like that. You know, first day on the job, orientation kinds of things. Fate played a different card.

As I opened the door to my new office and turned on the TV, I learned that an electrical blackout had shut down most of the East Coast. Frank Whittaker, the news director, knocked on the door.

"Don, would you like to go on the air with this?"

I didn't hesitate.

"Yes," I said. "Of course."

Instead of meeting the staff, doing the paperwork and having orientation, I ended up co-anchoring a two-hour live broadcast before *The NBC Nightly News* took over, and then picked up again with a thirty minute newscast after *The Nightly News*. I even managed to get friends and New York City officials to do live phone interviews with me to tell the audience about what they were experiencing.

Welcome to Chicago.

I had hoped this move would finally give me the chance to pursue the kinds of stories that interested me with greater freedom. Instead, I ran into my old nemesis once again, the black box. The box and I geared up for another round together on low expectations of what viewers will want to hear about, and what stories are worth telling.

CHAPTER 12

A Lesson in Priorities

What we have in our lives is a direct result of what we deem important—our priorities. If your family is important, it shows in the way you allocate your time and money. If your career is important, it gets the time and money. Most of us understand that we *get* the most from those areas of our lives where we *give* the most.

You might be surprised to know that the same rules hold true in an evening newscast. Time and money are allocated toward certain information and certain audiences. These facts are something that became a greater issue for me while working for WMAQ in Chicago.

I've always lobbied for the stories that I believed would be interesting and important, but in Chicago, I realized that I was going to have to find ways to reach beyond traditional journalism to get certain stories told. I learned that the best way to convince others to change their priorities was to act fully on my own.

That New Guy From the Network

When I arrived at at WMAQ in the fall of 2003, I'll admit I probably was a little cocky. After all, I'd been working in a big national forum for almost two years, and had earned an Edward R. Murrow Award, one of the highest awards in journalism. I had been swimming in a pretty large pond, filled with "big fish," like Andrea Mitchell, David Gregory, Tom Brokaw and Katie Couric. Chicago is a huge city with millions of viewers in its local news audience, but compared to NBC, it was a small pond where I thought I could be a big fish.

Yes, I know how this sounds, but the title of this book is *Transparent* for a reason. When my ego gets a little out of control, I have to cop to it. I think that might have been the case when I first arrived in Chicago. I definitely had the feeling that my new co-anchors viewed at me with a degree of skepticism and wariness.

I may have unintentionally proved them right by jumping into my first editorial meetings with a list of stories that *I* wanted to do that contradicted their long-held beliefs about what their audience wanted.

I guess that wasn't my most diplomatic moment.

On the other hand, some of the stories that my colleagues resisted, and that I found ways to do anyway, ended up being extremely popular with the local viewers. It was also some of the best work of my career. It's not that I was right and they were wrong. It's just that more often than not, I have a different way of looking at the world than most people. I also think, more often than not, that viewers appreciate being taken out of their comfort zones.

By the time I left Chicago three years later, my work there had been rewarded with four Emmys. I also had lots of run-ins with my colleagues at WMAQ, which was a new experience for me. Steel sharpening steel?

Maybe.

"People don't want to hear about AIDS —it's depressing."

This was the reaction when I proposed a story on HIV/AIDS at my new Chicago home.

You bet it's depressing. It's a horrible disease that, in spite of a number of successful treatments, still has no cure. That's one reason we should all care about it.

Here's another one—right now, AIDS is affecting the African American community at a disproportionally high rate. According to the Centers for Disease Control, approximately 1.1 million

Americans are afflicted with this deadly disease. Almost half of them, 46%, are Black Americans. Considering that Black Americans are only 12% of the entire population, this is an astounding, and dangerous, statistic. It's significant enough that in June 2010, the Office of National AIDS Policy had a meeting at the White House solely focused on the epidemic of HIV cases among African American men.

The stigma associated with AIDS in the black community is very high. Although HIV/AIDS has proven to be an equal opportunity killer of blacks, whites, gays and straights, men and women, it's still perceived as a homosexual disease. The black community still shows a high degree of intolerance for its gay brothers and sisters.

Those were some of the reasons my station didn't want to touch my story ideas about AIDS with a ten foot pole.

Unfortunately, I'd heard those arguments before.

In 2002, while at NBC News, I pitched, shot and edited a story about HIV/AIDS in the black community. The story focused on a Miami church that had made the bold move of embracing people with HIV/AIDS, reaching out to be of service to a community of people that many black churches had traditionally shunned. The producers for both *Today* and *Nightly News* loved the story, but it never aired.

Why?

They felt it wasn't a story suited for either program's audience or demographic, as we say in the TV business. The core audience of both shows was older, white Americans in general, with

Today garnering mostly older white women. Along with being "big-footed," which means pushed to the margins by more well-known journalists, seeing our stories languish without ever being aired was a frustration that many of the minority journalists at national news organizations like NBC News shared. While we were honored to be working side by side some of the heavy-hitters in our business, we were frequently frustrated because our story ideas and input were often overlooked or dismissed because news managers either did not understand, appreciate or welcome stories which affected or were important to minorities. There was no real solution. We were left with the choice of either "grin and bear it" and keep trying, or speak up and risk being labeled as difficult or trouble makers.

So while NBC News loved my HIV/AIDS story, they never aired it because they didn't think it would appeal to an audience that was more interested in stories about hormone replacement therapy, low testosterone for men or senior citizens who gamble too much.

This is just the reality of the priorities that come with who is the audience, who advertisers are paying to reach and the amount of time available in a broadcast.

Want to test it out?

The next time you watch the evening news, pay close attention to the commercials. The commercials tell you *exactly* who the program is aimed at. The stories in the broadcast, other than the breaking news of the day, will be aimed at exactly the same people as the commercials.

Here's another example of how minority-centered coverage works in real life:

Remember when the great soul singer Luther Vandross had a massive stroke in April 2003? He lingered in a coma for two years before passing away in July 2005. I reported on the stroke in 2003, and simultaneously, prepared a story on his life, just in case he died. While that may seem premature, it's not uncommon in the news business. We call them "obits" and they are already "in the can" for almost every major celebrity, especially the older ones like Betty White, the sick ones like Michael Douglas, or the troubled ones like Whitney Houston, Lindsay Lohan and Charlie Sheen. There are also pre-prepared obits for politicians. Barack Obama, Bill Clinton, George Bush and Jimmy Carter all have them.

While working on these stories for Mr. Vandross, the producer and I discussed interview possibilities. Who should we talk to get a background of his career and music? She suggested someone from *Rolling Stone Magazine*. I suggested *Vibe* magazine. After all, I think of *Rolling Stone* as more rock and roll or mainstream music. Since Luther had started out as a soul singer and then "crossed over," I felt a *Vibe* reporter would be able to give more nuance to the life of a man with a legendary career.

To my surprise, the producer refused to even consider using a writer from *Vibe*.

Just refused.

"No," she said with a surprising finality.

You know how I feel about that word.

So I pressed her.

"Well," she sarcastically replied. "We don't want to make this a *black* story, do we?"

I was dumbfounded. All these years of being a Luther Vandross fan, and somehow I had failed to realize that he *wasn't* a black man. After all, once he crossed over musically, he somehow ceased to be *black*, right? And since he wasn't black anymore, we couldn't do make our story about him have any *black* people in it talking about him, could "we?"

How silly of me—thinking Luther Vandross was black!

Okay, I know I've indulged heavily on the sarcasm here, but you see the problem minorities in broadcasting face. News organizations want their stories to appeal to a broad cross-section of people and there's a fear that if the coverage is too minority-oriented, too black, in these cases, it will miss the mark and lose the audience.

Once again, this is not an easy rail to ride. I feel obligated as a black man to try to present stories that will interest people who look like me, but getting those stories on the air can be incredibly difficult.

When I first joined WMAQ, I had big hopes. I had all kinds of stories that had been rejected by NBC News, and I carried these story ideas with me from New York to Chicago, determined to somehow get them on the air and bring some light to some dark places. In Chicago, I would be the big fish, or so I thought, and would be able to take more of my stories to the air and let the viewers decide. I had been promised the chance to have more control over what kinds of stories I worked on. I had been promised that as a former network anchor and correspondent, I wouldn't be running around the city, covering the crime beat.

Ha.

Before long, I realized that the promises that I'd be working primarily on "big" stories, special reports and investigations would not be kept. I was even suspended once for questioning why I was constantly being sent to cover shootings and stabbings, the crime beat, instead of the work I was hired for!

I'm not saying that crime stories aren't important. They are vitally important to most communities. The problem is that they rarely require much from a journalist in terms of writing or reporting skills. Sending me, with all I had learned from my experiences with NBC News, out to cover a shooting was like sending a tank out to break up a fight between a couple of kindergartners. It was truly a waste of my talent and experience.

I was frustrated and disappointed. I was also more than a little angry, but I didn't give up. I couldn't. *I wouldn't.* I knew I would find a way to do the stories I wanted to do, including the HIV/AIDS story, one way or another.

You're probably thinking that the reason I was so determined is because I'm gay.

It's not, even though some at the station thought that, too.

My colleagues told me that they, and the management, were only looking out for my best interests by continually rejecting my HIV/AIDS story ideas. They thought that viewers would question my sexuality or wonder if I had AIDS. I listened, but dismissed their arguments. It was absurd. Everyone in our business has, at one time or another, reported on issues that have nothing to do with their own personal lives. To me, the stigma and fear associated with the topic, even within our own station, made it *even more* important for me to get out there and start the dialogue. I was not afraid of what people might say about me because I chose to report on HIV/AIDS. I may have been naïve. I may have been a little reckless, but I certainly wasn't afraid.

If anything, being *black,* rather than being gay, was the motivating force behind my determination to cover HIV/AIDS.

I felt that, as a black journalist, I had even more of an obligation to continue the focus. The CDC's statistics showing the disparate impact of the virus on the black community makes it very clear—HIV/AIDS isn't a gay disease. It's a *black* disease.

First, I pitched the idea of doing a local story about the threat of HIV/AIDS in Chicago. I wanted to talk to local organizations and find out how they were responding to it, what efforts were being made to educate people on avoiding infection and what kinds of treatments and facilities were available to those suffering with the disease.

"No," they said.

So then I started thinking about the global epidemic of the virus. AIDS was ravaging Africa and I thought perhaps that might be a better way to bring attention to the subject by discussing the plight of people half a world away into focus for our viewers. I hoped that telling the story from a global point of view, rather than a local one, would be an alternate way of delivering a message to those here who needed to receive it. I hoped that if I told the story with people of color, people who looked like me, I could not only shed some light on an epidemic problem in nations like Congo, Rwanda, Gambia and South Africa, but also on the epidemic problem right here in the United States.

I pitched the story that way.

"No," they said.

You know the joke about the kids on the long car ride who keep asking, "Are we there yet? Are we there yet?" Well, I kept asking, "Will you send me to Africa? Will you send me to Africa?" The response was always, "No, that's not something our viewers are going to be interested in. Stick to Chicago."

"But I wanted to do a story on AIDS in Chicago and you didn't want to do it."

"And we still don't. Next idea, please?"

Finally, I realized that the only way I was going to tell this story was to create the opportunity myself. I had to go to Africa on my own dime and time.

CHAPTER 13

A Lesson on Initiative

You know the famous lines from the movie "Field of Dreams"? I think the words are: "If you build it, they will come."

By deciding to travel to Africa myself, without the resources of a news organization, to tell stories about HIV/AIDS, I was paraphrasing those words into my own mantra—If I tell it, they will watch. Or at least that's what I hoped would happen as I spent my own free time and money to tell the story of HIV/AIDS from an African perspective.

The lesson for me was simply this—Sometimes taking the initiative really does pay off.

To Africa

Once I decided that I was going to tell an African HIV/
AIDS story on my own, I started doing some research, getting
in touch with people, and doing the advance work for my travels. I started with a doctor in the Chicago area who had done
some work in hospitals in Africa. Dr. Mardge Cohen was able
to put me in touch with a NGO, a non-governmental organization, in Rwanda. A friend of mine put me in touch with Matthew Bedella, an independent representative who worked with
Abbott Labs in providing HIV/AIDS medication to afflicted
people in African nations. Dr Mardge and Matthew helped me
put together story ideas, people to interview and places to visit
in several African nations. They advised me on securing drivers,
guides, and suggested other contacts that I would need to get the
stories I hoped to get while assuring that I'd have some measure
of security while travelling.

Once I had done as much planning as I could without the
help of a major news organization, I enlisted my friend John
Grkovic, an eager Columbia College film student, to travel
with me. I booked our flights to Africa myself. I bought all our
equipment—cameras, microphones, a computer, and software. I
probably spent $15,000 of my own money in preparations. This
is why I wanted the support of a news organization. It can get
expensive to be a citizen journalist, especially when one needs to
be able to submit a product equal to what is expected in a top
five broadcast market's evening news.

I got two weeks of vacation time and it was set. We were off.

It was a whirlwind trip. Four countries in two weeks—Kenya, Malawi, Rwanda and Tanzania. Our itinerary was loosely based on the contacts I had made in advance of our trip, but was ultimately dictated by who was available, and willing, to talk with us when we arrived.

We landed in Kigali, Rwanda knowing absolutely nothing, and having not much of a plan for what to do first and uncertain of what to expect. This was 2005, about ten years after the genocide that decimated the population there, and it was a complete culture shock in every way from the first moments. There were armed men and guns everywhere, more than I had ever seen in my life!

We weren't in Chicago anymore.

I took one look at John, a red-haired, fresh-faced white kid, and I knew he was thinking:

"What the hell have I gotten myself into?"

I was thinking the same thing myself, but I didn't say it. Something always kicks in for me in situations like this. I get very calm, very certain. You'd never know I am the slightest bit rattled from my outward demeanor.

It's a useful skill.

"We're going to get a taxi to the hotel," I told him, shouldering up my share of our bags of equipment and setting out like I knew what I was doing.

Ha.

It was a reasonable way to start our excursion, going to the hotel. We had travelled nearly 30 hours and we were completely exhausted. We should have been ready to collapse into a long, deep sleep, but it's a funny thing about travel and how excited you get when you finally arrive. When we got to the hotel, we were both too amped up to sleep.

"Let's just do this," I said.

John agreed.

We called a driver Dr. Mardge had recommended. Fortunately, he was available and met us at the hotel almost immediately. Off we went, in search of a story.

It was Sunday. We didn't know much about what was happening in the city until our driver told us about the soccer match, a big game between Rwanda and one of their bitterest rivals, Nigeria. Soccer is hugely popular in Rwanda and they have a pretty good team. We decided to go and check it out, hoping there might be a story there.

The traffic was unbelievable. The only way to describe Rwandan traffic is to imagine a crowd fleeing a charging bull at a bullfight. No defined lanes, no sense of order, just manic panic in all directions. There were no stop signs or stop lights and no police directing traffic. Drivers just navigate the streets the best way they can.

It's absolutely terrifying.

When we finally made it to the stadium parking lot, it too, was crowded. As soon as we exited the car, we were swarmed by dark, gleaming Rwandans staring at us, trying to touch John's light skin and hair. With my skin not quite as dark as theirs, some of them were even grabbing for me. We were both stunned by this attention, almost to the point of being frozen in our tracks, too uncertain of how to respond to move. Thankfully, our driver still had his presence of mind. He grabbed us and literally pushed us towards the security guards at stadium's entrance.

Of course, the game was sold out and there wasn't a ticket to be found. Sometimes, having a camera can get you in anyway, and sometimes having a camera will close the doors to you forever. We weren't sure which way it would go for us, but we took out our equipment and crossed our fingers.

Turns out the cameras, plus a few good old American dollars, got us escorted not just into the stadium, but *right onto the soccer field!* We were doubly lucky because the Rwandan president, Paul Kagame, and his wife were among the excited spectators. John and I didn't say a word to each other because we both knew we had a *great* story unfolding right there.

It's a slice of life we don't often see here in the United States, the joy and energy of a soccer match in an African nation. Usually, all the news we get of African countries is of suffering and war. This was something completely different, a fresh take on life on the continent. We treated it like that. That soccer match was something fresh. It was a new slice of African life, removed from the usual stories of strife, famine and disease. It was joyous and fast-paced and exhibited Rwandan national pride, especially when the Rwandan team beat the Nigerian team in overtime.

John and I shot the video of the match, of the president and his wife, interviewed a few people and returned to our hotel to put the story together.

We filed the story as a video blog, or vlog as these are known. A vlog is really just a diary of your personal experiences on video, and mine was done with the skill and professional acumen of a journalist.

While we had all the right equipment, software and know-how, our lack of network support caused problems that required us to be creative. We didn't have access to a satellite to beam our story back to the U.S., so instead, we edited the video on an Apple laptop loaded with video software, then uploaded it to U-Sendit.com where the files would be compressed enough to be sent over the Internet. The process took hours and the dial-up Internet connection available to us would often crash in the middle of sending the files. We were often forced to start the process all over again.

To keep the laptop from burning up, we'd place it atop an air conditioning vent to cool it off. God was smiling on us because the computer never crashed and the files, though excruciatingly slowly, always transferred—eventually. John and I spent many sleepless nights staring at the file transfer status bar on the computer screen watching our work slowly upload. It was our version of watching TV in Africa, and just like a good television drama or ball game, we exhaled with satisfaction at the end. Seeing the words "transfer complete" was like winning a championship. But would the viewers back in Chicago care?

We thought the first upload, the story of the Rwandan soccer match, was refreshing, unique and interesting. Back home, the station put our story up on its website. On the other side of the world, John and I, bleary eyed, road weary, and sleep deprived, waited and worried. The video was up, but had anyone bothered to look at it? There wasn't a single comment on the website. Not one.

I was beginning to think I'd traveled all the way to Africa only to prove the naysayers right.

Then, finally there was a comment. Then there were two comments. Ten comments. Thirty comments. Then hundreds of comments poured in! We were psyched. In our exhaustion, we failed to realize that our work was arriving and being posted in the middle of the night in Chicago. We had no concept of time or of the time difference. We were living in our own time, in the moment, not watching or being influenced by a clock.

The success of that first upload of the Rwandan soccer victory set the tone for the remainder of the trip. Viewers asked for more. The station wanted more. MSNBC.com even commissioned us to write an article for their website. I think you can still find it at http://www.msnbc.msn.com/id/8207378.

Sometimes by ourselves, sometimes with guides, John and I traipsed from African nation to African nation, submitting stories about AIDS, about relief efforts, about the how HIV was a legacy of the regions many wars, about life for the men and women and children who, after surviving so much, now faced yet another battle for medicines that might prolong their lives.

This is how it went for 14 days. John and I flew, walked and drove all over East Africa, chronicling the people, their cultures and our experiences for the audience back home. Most days, we had no real plan of what we would focus on or who we would talk with, but somehow we'd always stumble upon some miracle of a story like the little girl in an AIDS ward at the Nazareth Hospital outside Nairobi.

She had been at death's door until, finally, she got the anti-retrovirals (AIDS treatment drugs) she needed at the last minute. Her family was too embarrassed to tell anyone she had AIDS. Even after she developed skin lesions, malaria, pneumonia and jaundice, they refused to accept it. Even when it reached the point that the little girl was emaciated, had lost most of her hair and was too weak to move, they denied the severity of her condition, choosing to believe she could be cured through prayer and religious rituals. They were afraid they'd be ostracized by neighbors, friends and even other family members if the truth of her illness were discovered. When she slipped into a coma, her parents reluctantly dropped her at Nazareth and abandoned her.

The people at the hospital called her 'the miracle child' because they were certain she would die, but thanks to the generosity of the United States and President George W. Bush's AIDS initiative PEPFAR (President's Emergency Plan for AIDS Relief), the hospital had access to one of the most powerful AIDS drugs available at the time, Combivar, known as the AIDS drug of last resort. Dr. Thomas Macharia told me that even he thought little Christine was a "goner," and while he prayed for her, he didn't hold out much hope.

Just one day later, Christine became more alert. She opened her eyes. They didn't sparkle yet, but they were open and focused.

Slowly, she began talking to the staff. Soon, she began to ask for food—an appetite was another good sign. Christine started to put on weight, her hair started to grow, and her personality returned.

I've always been baffled by people who somehow think that spirit/religion and science are mutually exclusive. To me, Christine's recovery was clear evidence that the two work together, hand in hand.

While the miracle child was calm during the days, she often cried at night because she missed her family, as did another child in the hospital bed next to hers. When the child saw me, she got out of the bed and walked towards me, still crying. Without thinking, I bent down and scooped her into my arms. As I bounced her up and down, I remember saying to her, "You just need some love. You just need some love." And she did. She stopped crying immediately.

Leaving those two children at the Nazareth Hospital in Nairobi was one of the hardest things I've ever done. I think about them to this day. I can see why people who visit children in other countries sometimes end up adopting them and bringing them back to the U.S. I wanted to bring every child I met back with me. I also knew that, as a single man always on the go, it would have been impossible for me to actually care for them and give them the homes they needed.

Another day, at the Thika Orphanage and Hospital in Nairobi, we met Wyamaetha Wykugura, who lived in a one room hut with her four grandchildren. Their mother, her daughter, had died of AIDS. The five of them shared a space that was no bigger than my bathroom. There was no running water or electricity.

I felt moved to do something to help her. So Matthew Bedella, John and I hired some of the villagers and bought the supplies to build her a new hut. It took us one day to do it and cost about $1,000 U.S. dollars. The entire village helped. While the men dragged posts, hammered, nailed, cut and sawed, the women cooked us meals and brought us cold water. We finished just before sunset. Before we left, the villagers prayed for us before sending us on our way back to our hotel with all its amenities. As a result that experience, I don't complain as much about my accommodations, no matter how bad they might seem. I know now, for certain, that people need very few luxuries to live a happy life. Food, clothing, shelter, love and family—that's all we really need.

My African journey reaffirmed my belief in kindness and the human spirit. People were really willing to open their homes, their lives and their struggles to us, even though we were strangers with cameras.

Or perhaps *because* we were strangers with cameras.

Our Rwandan driver, Samuel was the source of a great deal of help and inspiration. He'd lost three aunts, two uncles, and all of his grandparents during the genocide. Many of his male friends were sick with or dead from AIDS. While we were traveling with him, he learned that his mother had been killed in a bus accident on a country road. He broke into a long wailing sob that seemed to go on forever.

I remember sitting next to him on the side of the road while he wept, thinking about the losses in my own life. I thought about my father and my stepfather. I thought of Mame, my grandmother.

Loss, grief, love, and joy—these are the things that unite us as human beings wherever we live on the planet. To remind others of that truth was a large part of why I wanted to go to Africa. Time and time again, we found connection and communion sharing those feelings with the people we met, as we did that day with Samuel when his mother died.

I remain deeply grateful to all the people who, in spite of their feelings of shame or pain or desperation, chose to talk to us. Almost of all of them did it because they wanted the world to know what was happening to them and to others like them around the world. They wanted to believe that their suffering might prevent someone else from the same fate. Everywhere, we found a richness of experience that resonated with the viewers back home.

When I finally returned, WMAQ ran a three-night series of the work John and I had done during my African travels. *NBC Nightly News* was lined up to air parts of my Africa footage, but Hurricane Katrina ripped through New Orleans that same week. The project was shelved, appropriately so, to cover that disaster.

My AIDS Africa stories also won two Emmys—one for the three-night series, another for our use of new media (the Internet) in covering the AIDS crisis in Africa. The real truth is that HIV/AIDS is an American story, not just an African one. It may not be pretty, and it may be depressing, and often it is desperately sad, but it's as important here as it is in Africa.

I hope I'm around and on the desk when it's announced that there's a cure for HIV/AIDS. It would be a moment in history I wouldn't want to miss.

CHAPTER 14

A Lesson Named "Katrina"

Hurricane Katrina brought me several lessons I never expected.

When the hurricane hit, once again I found that in order to get where I felt I needed to be, I had to be particularly focused and persistent. The crisis also gave me a deeper insight into how people come together in times of loss, and revealed my own dependence on what I consider our "normal, everyday life."

It also began something unexpected. It began to reconnect me to the South, to Louisiana and to my home.

I've Got to Go!

"I have to go. I have to. These are my people. I have to go."
Even I was surprised by the fervor and emotion in my voice.

It was August 30, 2005, one day after Katrina slammed into
the Gulf Coast, and I was pleading with my news director to be
sent down to New Orleans. Growing up in Baton Rouge meant
that I knew New Orleans and the Gulf Coast well. I was positive
I could bring something fresh to the coverage of the most disas-
trous hurricane to strike American soil in decades.

But what did they say?

No.

"No" because they already had someone down there.

"No" because it was being covered by affiliate reporters and it
wasn't necessary. "No" because of the presence of national media.

"No" because of the cost.

"No" because I was needed in Chicago.

Every "no" was like oil on a grease fire to me. I knew I was
getting to New Orleans one way or the other. I just needed to
figure out how. In the meantime, like a little kid determined to
nag his way into a new toy, a Happy Meal or whatever, I was in
and out of my news director's office begging.

"I gotta go. You gotta let me go. I can do something unique
with this. I'm from Baton Rouge, just 80 miles away. This is
practically in my backyard."

No.

Finally on September 1, three days after Katrina, and after
three days of repeated pestering, three days of coverage in which

the country and the whole world saw a level of suffering and devastation unlike anything we've ever imagined on American soil, my station finally let me go.

Persistence really is a virtue, and this is a lesson my life has taught me over and over again.

A videographer and I set out the very next day. By then, it was almost a full week after the disaster, and at long last some of the people who had been stranded at the Super Dome and the Convention Center were finally getting on the buses that would take them to cities all around the nation.

For many who had been following the saga, seeing those poor people finally boarding buses seemed to be the beginning of the end, but they were wrong. There were still plenty of stories to tell, if I could get down there.

My station had given me the green light, but I still couldn't *get* to New Orleans.

There were no flights into the flood-ravaged city. I couldn't get any flight anywhere *near* there. All the flights to nearby cities were booked with displaced people trying to return home and relatives trying to find out about loved ones affected by the storm. I waited on stand-by and finally got a flight to Mobile, Alabama a day later.

I wanted to hit the ground running. Unfortunately, that, too, turned out to be harder than I had expected.

We're all spoiled by how well things usually work in our society, but in a disaster, things that are usually no-brainers become extremely difficult. First, when I arrived, there were no rental cars available. When we finally got a car, there was no gas available, not just at the airport, but all over the region. Trucks had not been able to reach the area to deliver any. Ditto for food and water. Lodging? There wasn't any of that either. Hotels were closed and their staffs had fled to higher ground if they were lucky. When we were tired, we took turns sleeping in the back of the SUV we'd finally been able to score at the airport. As we drove toward New Orleans, we saw the lines of people at every gas station hoping to be able to buy gas, food, water and other supplies.

This is what life comes to when the infrastructure collapses. There's no grocery store, and there's no running water. There's no "flip on the TV and get the news." Instead, there are massive lines for the most basic necessities. Fortunately, on the Mississippi Gulf Coast those lines were orderly and civil, but when you're in the midst of disaster on the scale of Katrina, you can quickly see how fast order and civility can deteriorate into chaos.

We pulled over to talk to the people in the lines. We wanted to find out how they were holding up, if they'd seen any relief efforts yet, if their homes were still standing, and how they'd weathered the storm. Among those standing in line was a former professional football player whose career I was slightly familiar with. He was waiting, just like everyone else. Such is the equalizer of a crisis—money and fame don't help much when there's nothing much left to buy, when there isn't any phone service to call for help and the roads are mostly blocked or washed out.

The player told us he was worried about family members he

hadn't been able to reach. It was a story we heard over and over again, probably the most common thread through Katrina's devastation. "I can't reach family." "I haven't heard from family." "I hope my family is okay."

People talked about their homes, but they were much more worried about their loved ones. I kept thinking about Africa, about the parents who knew that they were dying of AIDS saying to us, "What about my family?" "Who will care for my family?"

Same words, different nations. Same words, different crisis.

Much as some would like us to believe differently, there really isn't any "us" and "them" in this world. We're all "us" with the same basic fears and hopes.

We left the gas station. We were driving through one of the neighborhoods near Gulfport just as a lady pulled up to what remained of her home. There wasn't much left. Her home was now just a jumble of rags, pieces and parts, wood, metal and glass. If you didn't know that it had once been a house, you might have thought it was a landfill or something. She got out of her car and just stood there, staring at it for a long time. Then, noticing us and the camera, she graciously allowed us to follow her story.

"We're all safe," she said after surveying the damage closely. Her sofa was in the front lawn and a neighbor's car was on her roof. Her car was gone. It had floated out to sea. The spectacle so chaotic it was almost comical. "This is all just stuff." She tried to smile, but I could see her eyes filling with tears.

Some people would call the moment exploitation. I would vehemently disagree. First of all, I'd never stick a camera in someone's face without their permission. If they don't want to be videotaped, we respect their privacy.

People say "yes" to being taped far more often than they say "no." They say "yes" because they know that telling their story helps in ways that are immediate and direct, and in more subtle and indirect ways, too. All through Katrina, the presence of journalists made the nation aware of the dire circumstances so many of our fellow Americans found themselves in. The results raised millions of dollars in relief funds for organizations like the American Red Cross and the Salvation Army. The results brought heavy pressure and scrutiny on government entities that didn't seem to have a response plan ready for those displaced by the high waters. The results were hundreds of volunteers from around the country and the world who flooded into New Orleans and the Gulf Coast to assist with the clean up.

It's not exploitation. Instead, it's an opportunity to give voice to what people are experiencing. Visual media is particularly powerful. Showing how little remained of this woman's home was an absolutely appropriate use of the platform of television.

A few months before Katrina hit, a local news anchor in Chicago on a different network, was alleged to have been involved in a serious scandal involving an inappropriate relationship with an underage girl. It was a really big local story and everyone was talking about it, trying to get information on what had happened, get the girl's story, and track whatever legal proceedings might result. The anchor had been suspended from his job, and he and his wife had basically gone into hiding. I told some of my colleagues that I was going to reach out to him, ask him for an interview and see what happened.

They all laughed at me.

"There's no way he's going to talk to you. He's not talking to anybody." They said, "If you get him to talk on air, that'll be one of the biggest gets ever. But he's not going to talk to you. Why should he?"

I called him. It took a few attempts, but at last I got the chance to talk with him.

"I know a lot of things are being said about you right now," I told him. "And I just wondered if you wanted a chance to tell your side of the story?"

He didn't say no. He talked it over with his wife and his legal representatives and called me back. "Thanks, Don. I'd like that very much," he said. A few days later they sat down with me and did the interview.

Journalists, whether they are holding cameras or notepads, help people give voice to what they are experiencing. That's our job. Sometimes it's an experience of joy, like the victory at the Rwandan soccer match. Sometimes, it's the experience of uncertainty, or loss, like the woman who returned after Katrina to find her home destroyed. Other times it's to allow people an attempt to explain themselves or set the record straight, like my news colleague from Chicago.

I'm sad to say that I never made it to New Orleans in the

initial aftermath of Katrina. My station refused to allow it for safety reasons, and rightly so. Most of my coverage was of the ravaged gulf coast of Mississippi. Getting to New Orleans was difficult because of the many flooded and damaged roads. There were concerns about our ability to safely get there and back, and then, there were the powers that be. My bosses wanted me back in Chicago, so after only a few days, I caught a plane and went back home.

Leaving bothered me. I didn't feel ready to leave. I wanted to get to Louisiana. I wanted to see New Orleans. As a native of Louisiana, I felt a little like I needed to check on the city, to see it for myself. It was like wanting to check on a relative—I couldn't rest until I saw for myself.

A week later, I took some of my vacation time and went back. This time, I didn't have a cameraman accompanying me, but it didn't matter. I took my personal camera and did more stories, and more vlogs about the efforts of re-building the city. I talked to people, some of whom I'd known since childhood, about the hurricane and how it had changed their world. I volunteered, helping to clear debris. Then, when my time was up, I took everything back to the station and said, "Here's what I did on vacation. Can we use it?" and they did.

Since then, I've been back to New Orleans every year to volunteer for at least a week. Sometimes I take cameras. Most times I don't because I'm there as a volunteer, not as a journalist. I feel like it's the least I can do as a native son of Louisiana. There is still a lot of work to be done to repair the city, and there are still a lot of angry, displaced people. I know all about the discrimination, the corruption and the ugliness of New Orleans. Katrina quite literally blew the roof off all of the underlying problems of the city and exposed them to the world. Katrina showed how few opportunities and safety nets there were for some blacks in New Orleans, and the few that existed were swept away by the flood waters.

It's been five years since Katrina and I still go back.

I keep going back because I don't want to forget what Katrina showed us about who gets attention in this country and who doesn't. Or what New Orleans is still teaching us about how systematic, institutional racism kills. It kills any hope of recovery for some people, and it wilts the hope of something better than the life they're living in other people. Still for others, it just kills. Literally. The murder rate in New Orleans was never America's proudest accomplishment, but right now it's among the most murderous cities in the nation. This is not really that surprising. People who had next to nothing now have even less. Since nothing better is offered, no education, no jobs, no sense of place or home, they turn to crime and drugs. The great American writer, James Baldwin, wrote that a nation is as racist as its institutions. What does it say about us that we've still done so little to rebuild for the poor and black residents of New Orleans?

So, on my vacations, I go. I volunteer with some of the local organizations that are still trying to rebuild all of the wards of the city. I go and I give people the opportunity to tell their stories. The stories I record there don't always get aired, but going is the least I can do. It's a way of making a personal connection to the people there because they need more than just checks and sympathy from us now. They want us to come to their restaurants, to come hear the bands play, and to buy the art and support their businesses.

They say you never fully appreciate something until it's gone. This proved true for me. After all those years being away from Louisiana, seeing the devastation after Katrina made me feel protective of the place where I grew up. I might not have wanted to live there, but that doesn't mean I wanted to see the place suffer.

The Hardest Working Man in Broadcasting?

Speaking of New Orleans brings up the subject of working over vacations.

I know it's weird, but I often work on my vacations.

In addition to volunteering, on some vacations I've spent the bulk of my time off teaching at my alma mater, Brooklyn College, working with the next generation of journalists. On other vacations, I have filled in for another broadcaster. I recently filled in on *The Tom Joyner Morning Show*, doing radio news briefs. I got up at 3:30 in the morning and, depending on where I was, I went to CNN Radio in New York or Atlanta or the local affiliate in Baton Rouge and pre-recorded an update—"This is CNN's Don Lemon, with your morning news." It took about an hour. When I was finished I went home and went back to bed.

I work so much because I love it. I love what I do, and I love opportunities to try new things. It's refreshing to have the chance to try something new or to challenge oneself with something different. I'm always looking for a new experience because with every experience comes a new perspective and a new story. This is what I thrive on.

Since I'm being transparent here, I'll have to admit there's more to it.

I feel uncomfortable with resting for too long. There are a lot of stereotypes about black men in my profession that I'm constantly rebutting. There's still an idea among some out there that "black talent," the on-air personalities that you see on television, aren't "real" news people. That we aren't serious journalists. That we're empty-headed "tokens" that networks have to hire to satisfy affirmative action requirements or signal to viewers that they respect "diversity." That stereotype casts all black broadcasters as less qualified and less hard-working. All we have to do is show up, read the words on the TelePrompTer and stay black.

I resent this.

I don't want there to be any mistake—I work my tail off. You know how Tom Joyner has that tag line about being the "haarrrdest working man in show business?" Well, I'll claim that title for the news business. I'm nobody's posable anchor doll, thank you very much. I'm always thinking. I'm always working.

If I had a family of my own, I know I'd have to become less career-driven. I'd have to learn to focus time on those relationships. I confess—the thought thrills me. I think I'd be a good father and it's something that I'd like to try one day.

I just don't know that today is the day.

So, I work. I work a lot and I struggle every day to cover the things that I think are important to people and the things they want to know.

Working hard pays off. People notice who's putting in the extra mile, who's being innovative and who's thinking beyond any kind of box. I know because in 2006, not too long after my African adventure and a couple of other stories I did while in Chicago won Emmys, CNN came courting again.

The timing was perfect.

Newspeople Get Laid Off, Too

Many people don't realize this, but news organizations have been as affected by the downturn in the economy as any other business sector. By mid-2006, things were starting to turn for WMAQ and many other stations and networks.

My station was forced to make a major reduction in force. Many of the reporting staff, both on and off air, was laid off. While I was spared that cut, the position I had been promised became unlikely to materialize. I could stay, but my opportunities for any kind of advancement would be limited. For me, there were additional considerations.

I had grown restless. I'd done well in Chicago. I'd won awards for some of my work, I loved the city and had gotten to see the rise of a local politician named Barack Obama from state senator to U.S. Senator. I'd also had my share of conflicts and problems. Besides, it just seemed like I was ready for something new. When CNN called, this time I was already mulling over my future and trying to decide what to do next.

I said "yes" to CNN and joined the cable news network in September 2006. I pulled up stakes and moved to Atlanta and began anchoring the daily afternoon newscasts.

PART FOUR:

My Life at CNN

CHAPTER 15

Inaugurating
Barack Obama

W orking for CNN the past several years has given me the best of both worlds in many ways. I'm a national anchor, which was my childhood dream, and I also have the opportunity to explore the stories that interest me, to interview people I find intriguing and to interact with viewers.

It's always difficult to analyze a situation while you're in it, and since CNN is my current situation, I can't offer up the same 20/20 assessment I've shared on other aspects of my life. What I can do, however, is tell you some really great stories about what it's like to work for one of the largest and most powerful news organizations in the world, and about some of the moments that have meant the most to me in my time here.

Perhaps one of the most historic was the inauguration of Barack Obama as our country's 44th President. Not only was that an amazing moment for me personally, but it also created yet another black box incident for me as journalist.

Bearing Witness to History

If you understand just a little of my background, you know why covering the inauguration of Barack Obama was one of the high points of my career. The inauguration of the first African American President was a pretty big deal for *all* the journalists who had the opportunity to attend, and there were plenty of them. For me, as a person, as a Black American man, Mr. Obama's election had another important symbolism. The inauguration of the first president who is also a man of color, was a deeply personal and satisfying moment for me as an American. Mr. Obama's election was a clarion moment for me, one that brought my own experiences, both personally and in my career, into sharp focus. In many ways, it was the moment that this book came sharply into focus in my mind. I was excited that a man whose unlikely career I had witnessed rise in Chicago—a Black American man who had defeated the stereotypes of the black box was now the President of the United States. I knew that one day he, too, would speak out on his experiences with the black box from his position and provide guidance to the next generation.

The Inauguration experience represented even more to me as a journalist. Bearing witness to Obama's election as an African American man in broadcast journalism, an industry that is still dominated by white men and women, gave me a unique perspective. The need for that minority perspective, in both politics and in the media, is part of what drives me to do what I do. It's so important that we, African American journalists, Asian-American journalists, Hispanic American journalists, Native American journalists, are here. This is important, not just for our own minority communities, but for the entire country. Diversity of point of view really is an American necessity, and nowhere is that more evident, in my experience, than in the media.

As I've said, Mr. Obama's inauguration was also another lesson in how "black box" thinking still affects me as a black journalist.

At the inauguration ceremony, Wolf Blitzer asked me my thoughts at that moment and I said something like, "As an African American man, with an African American mother at home who is watching this moment, and I know, crying, I am absolutely overcome."

It was completely spontaneous, completely serious and completely sincere. I didn't rehearse it, and it wasn't something I had written in advance and waited for the right moment to say. It was what came out of me, an African American man, who has experienced racism first hand and seen its affects on my family, my friends and my community, as I watched a black man being sworn in as President of the United States.

For some, my comments set off a black box moment. They automatically read into my remarks a preference for Mr. Obama because he is black, and for no other reason. Or because, as a journalist with CNN, I must have a liberal, Democratic bias. Neither is the case. My life experiences have taught me to see people as individuals, not as colors. Politically, in fact, there is no bias. I was involved with the Young Republicans for a while when I was in college and I am admirer of Ronald Reagan. None of this matters to those people. In their world, a black man commenting on seeing another black man inaugurated as President is a slam dunk for bias. They either can't understand, or don't want to understand. I'm not sure which.

I've quoted James Baldwin before, but it's appropriate to use his words again here. He wrote, "A nation is as racist as its institutions." To see a Black American in the Oval Office says something powerful about our institutions, and this is what was at the heart of my statement. Unfortunately, the political arena has become so divisive now that it's difficult for many people to remain objective. To my mind, the chasm between Republicans and Democrats seems purposeful. There's black and white, so to speak. No gray. The right side and the wrong side, without any middle ground that acknowledges either side has a valid point. There's no place in our political landscape for people who are conservative on the need to balance budgets and limit taxation, but who are more liberal on social issues, or for any other mix of conservative and liberal ideologies. Our political system fails to register the gray areas. Instead, it thrives on fighting.

Most Americans seem to be annoyed by this and it shows in the way people respond to those who are in power. Is there a point where conservatives, especially fiscally, can make a lot of sense? Sure there is, but that's not the exclusive realm of Republicans. Bill Clinton, a Democrat, balanced the federal budget, trimmed expenses and ended his eight years in office with a surplus, while Republican Presidents have talked about it and then have not done it. Some criticism there seems fair to me. I would offer that the same applies when Republicans successfully tackle social issues in ways that end up improving the lives of minorities. Both credit and criticism should be given where they are due.

In the interest of full transparency about my comments about Mr. Obama, I admit we do have a history. I first met him in 2003 when he was in the Illinois State Senate and I was a new anchor with Chicago's NBC affiliate. We seemed to always be at the same charity events, usually something sponsored by a local civil rights leader like the Reverend Jesse Jackson or black business luminary like Linda Johnson Rice.

When he announced his plans to run for U.S. Senate, no one expected him to win. Since I was working in Chicago at the time, I covered parts of that election, and when I tell you "no one expected him to win." I mean that winning would have been like a 90 degree day in the depths of January in that part of the world!

Everyone figured he was just making a "practice run" and in the end, he'd lose and return to the Illinois Senate, where he had become chair of the Health and Human Services Committee and seemed to be doing well.

Mr. Obama is nothing, if not determined, as we all know now. He was the underdog, most in the black community did not support him and there was a whole field of other Democratic candidates in the race. Somehow, scandal and controversy eliminated the other hopefuls one by one. When the dust settled after the primary in March 2004, Barack Obama was the only one left standing. Then his Republican adversary, Jack Ryan had to drop out of the race after revelations about some bizarre sexual escapades involving cages, whips and his ex-wife. Desperate for a substitute candidate, the Illinois GOP imported Alan Keyes, a respected black conservative who wasn't even from Illinois.

Obama won the Senate seat.

By the time Obama announced his candidacy for the Presidency in 2008, I had left Chicago and was an anchor with CNN.

I covered some of Mr. Obama's campaign for President at CNN, but not as much as the political unit—Wolf Blitzer, Candy Crowley and others. Politics wasn't my beat, but after he won, I knew wasn't going to let history pass me by without being a part of it. I called my contacts with the Obama campaign, got press credentials, and convinced my executive producer, Jennifer Bernstein, to allow me to go and cover it for my weekend, prime-time newscasts.

Once there among the CNN staff, there was no real distinction between who was there from the political unit and who was there for general coverage. We were all covering the moment, commenting on it, feeling its significance.

Since the Inauguration, covering Mr. Obama has caused me more than my fair share of headaches and criticism. Since I'm a Black American, it's assumed that I'm automatically his fawning admirer. It's assumed that I'm utterly incapable of having any objectivity about his presidency or of any critical thought about his policies. When I do interviews involving Mr. Obama's policies or about his speeches or actions, the black box filters every question through its narrow, racist prism and spits back the rallying cry: "Favoritism!"

This is blatantly unfair. I'm absolutely certain that if the same questions and comments I ask about Mr. Obama were asked by a white reporter, they would be heard differently. The black box filters would be lifted and maybe, just maybe, a question could just be a question.

Then there are those who hear a criticism of the President in every question or comment I make. Through their own version of the black box, these folks hear betrayal and they demand to know why I insist on attacking Mr. Obama. Why can't I be happy to see a member of my own race doing such an important and difficult job? Why won't I just leave him alone?

I can't win.

Whether it's coming from a white person or a black one, black box thinking is reductionist at best. They're reducing the person, in this case, me, down to their own preconceived notions about what he must believe without giving him a chance to show his individuality. Now sure, everyone does it. Our culture is filled with "boxes" and categories, each with their own distinct lists of characteristics. Think of rednecks and good ol' boys. Or Valley girls and computer geeks. Or soccer moms and punk rockers. There are plenty of boxes for white people, so many that we don't even call it a "white box" because we know that there's no unity of opinion in it, but even these other boxes, these cultural stereotypes, are wrong. You know it if you've ever tried to neatly fit someone into one. It never works. We're all so much bigger than that.

For the record, I'm not a Democrat or a Republican. If I had to classify myself (and in truth, I would prefer not to) I would either say that I'm not political or that I'm an Independent, reserving the right to choose the candidate from any party whose platform is most similar to my own. There are things I admire about certain Republicans I've talked with, and things I admire about certain Democrats that I've met. I'm still a great admirer of Ronald Reagan. As a journalist, a communicator, I loved his skill in that arena. They didn't nickname him "The Great Communicator" for nothing. The man was a master, but there were policies he advocated that I disagreed with and feel were particularly harmful to minorities and gay people. I can disagree with some of his policies and still admire his speaking ability.

That's my attitude toward politics. I'm not dependent on the tenets of a particular ideology. I don't lean to the left or right, ideologically. Allowing a political affiliation to completely define who you are and what you believe is too simple for me. It's like wearing only one suit, which is something I couldn't imagine ever doing as long as I had a choice.

CHAPTER 16

A Lesson on the Brevity of Life

I t's a tired cliché that "life is short," and yet there are moments when the brevity of life, and the suddenness and unexpectedness with which it can end, brings that old saw into sharp clarity. The death of music superstar Michael Jackson drove that message home for a lot of people all around the world, and I was one of them.

First, in the interest of full disclosure and transparency, I am a Michael Jackson fan. I use the present tense on purpose. Michael's death did nothing to change my appreciation for him or his music. I believe he was genius and a true pioneer on a number of fronts, including, almost accidentally, in the Civil Rights Movement. Indeed, I am such a fan that on the first day of pre-school, I took my Jackson Five album "ABC" to school to show the other kids, and it was stolen. I was so heartsick that my mother bought me another copy. My sisters and I would dance around and pretend we were the Jackson Five.

I was in Chicago when the news came of the death of the King of Pop, doing an event tied to the *Black in America* special with Soledad O'Brien. We had just arrived in Chicago and were headed to the event when we heard the news. A bit later, one of the producers said to me, "Jon Klein is trying to get in touch with you." Jon was the president of CNN US. Having Jon looking for you is sort of a big deal, so I tried to send him an email, but I couldn't.

My phone was so jammed with emails, I couldn't use it. I couldn't figure it out. I couldn't erase the messages. I couldn't listen to them. I couldn't do anything. The device was just stuck, so I borrowed a phone and called immediately. I suspected they wanted me to go to LA and cover the death of the King of Pop, and there was nothing I wanted to do more.

I'd spent years in Chicago and I knew that if I was going to LA, I'd need to get out of there now. It was already almost six o'clock and I knew that the last flight to the West coast usually departs from O'Hare at around 7 pm, but the phones were conspiring against me. Mine was dead, and I was having trouble reaching the right people in Atlanta with my borrowed device.

Finally, I got through and heard exactly what I expected:

"Get on a plane to LA as soon as you can."

Our driver had just left but I called him back.

"Get me to the airport, fast," I told him. "I have to get on the last plane to LA. It leaves in an hour."

In rush hour traffic, which in Chicago, like most major cities, is often a nightmare, we somehow got from the Southside of the city to O'Hare International Airport in 45 minutes. I remember urging the driver to "drive like a New Yorker, drive like a New Yorker." I'd finally been able to reach the tech guys and my phone was working again, so the whole time I was in the backseat, I was on the phone, trying to get a flight. From my years as a Chicago news anchor, I had a contact at United Airlines who I was pretty sure could help me.

She did. United hooked me up, but they warned me it was going to be really, really close.

It *was* really close. In spite of the driver's best efforts, I got there within minutes of the flight taking off. The person I'd spoken with on the phone knew I was en route, and that it would be really close. They opened a courtesy ticket window for me where they literally handed me my ticket, escorted me through security and then I did an OJ Simpson Hertz commercial (when he was an adored sports personality and before he was a social flashpoint and pariah) and literally ran to the gate. Just as I got to the gate, the agent took my ticket and closed the door behind me. I called Jon and told him I made it. He said, "Go get 'em."

I arrived in LA in the middle of the night. I was amped up and not really tired at all. Even if I *had* been tired, it wouldn't have mattered. It was after one in the morning in Los Angeles, but the news business is geared toward the East Coast morning shows which begin around 7 am ET. This meant that I was scheduled to have a live broadcast from the County Coroner's office, where Michael Jackson's body had been taken, in less than three hours, so instead of going to the hotel, I pointed my rental car toward the coroner's office.

I had no idea where I was going. I'm not really all that familiar with LA and I had only a rough idea of where I was headed. When I started seeing people standing in the street holding candles, I knew I was in the right place. Even in the middle of the night, there were all these people in the street. There were people everywhere, holding a vigil for the singer. I drove around slowly, taking it all in, then I went to the hotel, closed my eyes for an hour or so, got up and went back to set up for the morning show live shots.

Every now and then, as a reporter, there's a moment when you understand that you can take ownership over an event and that you can really become someone whose information is seen as particularly credible or as the "go to" person for what's happening on the scene. I felt that way about the Michael Jackson story. Very quickly, I really realized that it was my story to have because many of the reporters didn't have any connection to the music or to the social fabric that was woven into every note, every line of Michael Jackson's songs. Then there were all these other connections. For example, not many people knew that Jermaine Jackson, Michael's brother, is a member of the Chicago-based, Muslim religious group, the Nation of Islam. Thanks to my years in Chicago, I knew the organization well, and I knew its leader, Louis Farrakhan. I knew the Rev. Jesse Jackson, who was close to the family and was in town to offer support and condolences. I also knew Rev. Al Sharpton, who ultimately became the Jackson family's media spokesperson. I knew them all well enough to be able to call and ask what was going on and be viewed as trustworthy and not just as another prying reporter on the phone.

In the vernacular of journalism, I had the "scoop" on the story.

I also got a brief interview with Joe Jackson at the BET Awards a few days later.

I was stationed outside the Shrine Auditorium in Los Angeles, hoping to capture some comments of the famous people attending the event about Michael Jackson and his legacy. When I got word that Joe Jackson, Michael's father, was coming by, I was truly excited to have the opportunity to ask him about how the family was doing.

It had been pretty common knowledge that Michael Jackson and his father hadn't gotten along well while Michael was alive. Michael had accused him of physical abuse and portrayed him as a tyrant who had pushed all of his children toward stardom, at the cost of their childhoods and their happiness. The relationship between Michael and his father had been strained to say the least, and most fans knew this.

I was live on the red carpet, cameras rolling and when Mr. Jackson walked up I asked, "Tough time for the family?"

"Yeah. And?" He shot back, already angry as though the question offended him.

I was stunned. It wasn't the reaction I had expected. I'd only asked one question and already the interview had already taken a big turn into Strangeville, so I did what I usually do when things get weird in interviews:

I shut up and let the silence speak. I let the microphone hang there for a long second or two and waited.

In the ensuing silence, it seemed to dawn on the Jackson patriarch that the cameras weren't props and that he was on live television.

"The family is doing fine," he said in a less hostile tone.

When I asked him if he had a comment on his son and his legacy, Mr. Jackson had a publicist step up to the microphone to read a prepared statement in which he and his wife asserted "authority" over Michael Jackson's music, his estate and his children. He said that they had retained an attorney to look into the final moments of his son's life. A moment later, the attorney appeared to reiterate what was already common knowledge: that the family had concerns about the circumstances surrounding Michael Jackson's death. Joe Jackson stepped back into frame to say that the family was fine, considering they had lost a "superstar."

Then he shocked me once again by dropping the subject of his son altogether to introduce someone named "Marshall" and began talking about his new record company, Ranch Records, which would be distributing music videos via Blu-Ray DVD.

The next day, the Rev. Al Sharpton appeared on *Anderson Cooper 360* and offered an explanation for Mr. Jackson's comments. According to Rev. Sharpton, on the red carpet entering the BET Awards Mr. Jackson had been asked about his upcoming projects and was responding to that question. Anderson pointed out that I had not asked him that question, which of course I hadn't. Mr. Sharpton's reply was that he wasn't familiar with my interview, but that he understood that, given the confusion of the presence of so many reporters and interviews on the red carpet, it was understandable that Mr. Jackson answered a question he hadn't actually been asked.

Make of that what you will. Both my interview with Mr. Jackson and Anderson Cooper's interview with Rev. Sharpton are still online at CNN.com. Those interviews are still available because of the extraordinary level of interest the entire *world* had in this story. I hadn't seen the planet as transfixed by a story since Barack Obama's inauguration. Hurricane Katrina and the Indonesian tsunami had that same compelling, can't-look-away level of interest, and because of the allegations of pedophilia, because of his plastic surgeries, because of the sheer strangeness of his life and times, Michael Jackson was a very polarizing personality. Whether you loved him or you hated him, you were following the story. Even people who had only negative comments about what had happened and the circus that surrounded it were still watching.

I was on CNN's *Reliable Sources* with Howard Kurtz when he did a show focused entirely on the question of the coverage of Michael Jackson's death and whether it had been too much or too little. Kurtz took the point of view that it was "over coverage" and the media was on a feeding frenzy on the subject. Since I had been covering the story since it broke, Howie asked me if I thought "deep down" that we were overdoing it.

"No," I said promptly. "And I consider those who say otherwise to be elitist."

Sparks flew after I said that, but here's the context:

By the time we did that panel on Howard Kurtz's show, there had been almost two weeks of coverage of Michael's death from every possible angle. I reminded them that Michael Jackson was an accidental civil rights leader, in music and music videos. Remember, it was Michael Jackson who integrated MTV and the world of music videos with "Beat It" in 1983. Until then, videos of black musicians were relegated to BET. The whole Jackson family story is an encapsulation of the American Dream: a dirt-poor family from Gary, Indiana rises to become a dynasty in American music. It's the sort of Cinderella tale that most Americans love and never tire of.

Viewed through those lenses, the coverage was not overdone and I said so. The people who felt that the story was in media overkill were generally people who didn't feel any connection to pop music, to the quintessential "American-ness" of the Jackson story, or to the tabloid feel of the coverage took on as the weeks rolled by. That tabloid feel was happening because people *wanted* to watch every aspect of the investigation into the musician's death, every aspect of the public outpouring of grief and every aspect of his being laid to rest. That was why the ratings were through the roof. People were deeply and sincerely *interested.*

My choice of the word "elitist" brought me all kinds of criticism, and that's fine with me. Like it not, news isn't high brow all of the time. Sometimes pop culture just takes over. Much as we'd like to think that viewers only care about the "important" stories, such as war, disaster, politics, and economics, sometimes it's pop culture that grabs and holds our attention. Sometimes the top stories are moments of history, and not world history, but pop history, like the deaths of Princess Diana, John Lennon, Anna Nicole Smith and Michael Jackson.

What's interesting is that the journalism professor and media critic on Howie's panel agreed with me. *Baltimore Sun* television critic and Goucher College professor David Zuriwak said that Michael Jackson embodied a number of conflicts and contradictions in our society about race, about gender, about music, about culture. Eight out of ten African Americans wanted news on that story, and plenty of other people all around the world felt the same, but his comments raised no eyebrows. Mine ignited a firestorm.

I can only feel that this, once again, points out how being an African American changes how certain words are perceived by the viewing audience. A white media critic and black journalist saying what amounts to the same thing are heard very differently.

It's the black box in action.

Covering the death of Michael Jackson was one of the most intense, non-stop experiences of my career. It was literally go, go, go for three weeks with very little time to rest. I hope it doesn't sound strange or macabre to say I loved it because I truly did love it. I loved it because I loved Michael Jackson's music, but also because I'm addicted to that kind of high energy moment. It's like a drug. I got teased on Howard Kurtz' panel about getting no sleep while covering Michael Jackson and that was no exaggeration, but a lack of sleep is something I have in common with the late King of Pop. He was a terrible insomniac and so am I.

I'm not ready to try a Propofol drip, but I know what it feels like to be exhausted and really need to sleep and to not be able to. It's frustrating and emotional and terrible to lie there, night after night with your mind spinning like a hamster on a wheel. I envy people who just turn out the light and close their eyes. It rarely happens like that for me. I'm not interested in taking anything. I want to be fresh and alert for anything that might happen, so I lay awake, watching Turner Classic Movies, *Law and Order* reruns or some other silly thing, hoping that sheer boredom will ultimately put me to sleep.

I sometimes think that the insomnia is one of the side effects of doing what I do. I never had trouble sleeping before my career got started in earnest. When I was working my way through college, I had lots of different jobs and plenty of stress because I was constantly struggling. Some semesters I'd work full time and go to school part time. Other times I'd work full time and go to school full time, too. As hard as that was, it was different. When

I was tired, I slept. Now, just like the King of Pop, I have a really hard time with getting to sleep.

Of course, I had a darker, more personal connection to another element of Michael Jackson's story. As everyone knows because of two widely-publicized accusations, Michael Jackson was accused of molesting children at his Neverland Ranch. The first accusation, made in 1993, was settled out of court for $22 million at the request of Jackson's record company, although Jackson and his attorneys wanted to proceed to trial. Many of those close to Jackson say he was completely innocent of the charges, and there were suggestions that the boy's family saw the accusations as a means of financial gain. In the second case, criminal charges were brought against Jackson in 2005. He was ultimately acquitted.

I've often thought about those children and their parents. If the accusations were false, I've wondered what kind of parents would launch their child into such a terrible position of testifying to the horror that is childhood sexual abuse. If the allegations were true, I admire the kids for their courage. That kind of confrontation is something I never did with my own abuser. I wonder what difference it might have made in his life, and in mine, if I had.

Covering the life of Michael Jackson stirred my own memories. I can't imagine what it would be like to be accused of child molestation if one were innocent. I can't imagine that my childhood idol, still a kid himself when I took his record with me to preschool in 1971, could be guilty of such a terrible act. I can't imagine accusing someone of something so heinous if it weren't true. I wonder how one lives with one's self if one has done that kind of harm to a child.

Reconciling my own feelings about my past has been a slow process. While therapy has helped, like many survivors of childhood molestation, I find it hard to become close to people. I find it hard to trust. I feel myself to be "different" in ways that aren't always good. Though I've done my best to erase the shame by talking about it, and by trying to understand what happened and why, and even to find some measure of forgiveness for the boys who perpetrated it, I know the experience has had negative ramifications for me, especially in terms of relationships.

As I've said, everything happens for a reason. I may never know the purpose of enduring that kind of trauma, but I sometimes catch a glimpse of the gifts of surviving it. For instance, I'm not afraid of very much. I never really thought about it before, but I've taken some real chances in my life and my career, like leaving Louisiana for New York with no job, no apartment and only $200 in my pocket, hopping on a flight to Rwanda without a news organization behind me or a clue about exactly what I'd do when I got there, standing in the winds of a hurricane with nothing but a windbreaker and microphone, cruising around the metro Washington area during the sniper attacks, and while I'll admit to being nervous, those feelings never kept me from jumping into the circumstances with both feet.

I guess I'd already survived my worst nightmares. What more was there to fear?

The other gift left by surviving that horrific period of my life is empathy. I'm able to connect with people who are going through all kinds of suffering. I get what they're going through, I really do. People respond to me. They open up and talk to me because they know I *know*. It's unspoken, but it's real. It's something that can't be faked.

CHAPTER 17

A Lesson on Listening

Gertrude Leblanc is a little old lady that I met as she was sitting on her porch in the Ninth Ward in New Orleans. I was there covering the five year anniversary of Hurricane Katrina. She's nobody famous, just a lady who went through the hurricane and lived to tell it. She reminded me of my grandmother, so I just went up and started talking to her. She'd been living in New Orleans in a house in the Ninth Ward for 47 years. Her husband had passed away years before Katrina. She wanted her house back, one with a bigger porch, for better sitting, and a bigger swing for better rocking.

"I know Brad," she told me just in passing, as though we'd been talking about someone of that name. For a second I thought this otherwise lucid-seeming old woman might have a touch of dementia.

"Brad?" I asked politely. I had no clue who she was talking about. She looked at me like *I* might have a touch of dementia, went into her house and got her photo album.

"Brad and me," she said, pointing to a picture.

There was Gertrude LeBlanc and beside her, smiling broadly, was movie idol Brad Pitt who has been doing a lot of great work rebuilding homes in New Orleans through a foundation he started.

"Oh . . ." I said, appropriately impressed. "*That* Brad."

People often ask me about the best interviews I've ever done, but they are usually disappointed with my answers. They're expecting me to say Oprah or Obama or someone like that, but the truth is that my best interviews are usually of just everyday people who've been caught up by an extraordinary circumstance. The lesson I've learned is that listening, really listening, to what people are saying is far more important than firing off questions. The lesson of interviewing is to just be quiet and let them talk.

A recent example is Shirley Sherrod. You remember her. She's the Department of Agriculture employee who was fired from her job when a certain conservative blogger ran video of her in which she seemed to express anti-white sentiments. It subsequently came to light that the video had been heavily edited and her words taken out of context. Instead of a message of racism and exclusion, she'd actually been talking about racial inclusion and the importance of reaching beyond our country's still unresolved issues about race. In the thick of the maelstrom surrounding her termination and the subsequent revelations about the truth of her remarks, I had the chance to interview her.

The woman was *fearless.*

I loved her. She revealed herself to be a person who acts completely in accord with her own personal moral compass. She cannot be cowed, threatened or dissuaded. She doesn't do what people expect her to do. She doesn't do things for money. She wasn't a placeholder or a pawn to be moved in anyone's game. Power and fame held little seduction for her. She wanted to do what was *right,* nothing more and nothing less.

I admired her. I admire people who stick to what feels right to them in the face of incredible pressures, and who don't do things when it feels wrong, no matter what the incentives. With all the people taking potshots at her reputation, all the people who wanted to take her down, she just stood her ground. I'm not sure I have that degree of steadfastness, but I'd like to. She's a pillar of strength. I admire that.

In my four years at CNN, there have been so many great interviews that it's gotten hard to keep track of them all. Another one that I remember particularly well was the one I did with 2010's winner of the South Carolina Democratic Senatorial nomination, Mr. Alvin Greene.

Some people thought I was being condescending to him, but that wasn't my intention. What some heard as condescension was my genuine concern. The guy gave so many slow, monosyl-labic answers that I finally just had to ask him:

"Are you all right? Are you sure? Are you impaired in some way?"

And his answers:

"Yeah. I'm okay. I'm sure. I just. . . ." He caught himself on the brink of a revelation and stopped. It was the first time he sounded like a politician in the whole interview. "I'm okay," he finished.

Here's the thing people who are reluctant or cagey about being interviewed don't understand: They tell us a whole a lot about themselves by what they refuse to say. Greene was a per-fect example. If he'd just come out and said, "Don, I don't know why I did this. I really didn't expect to win, I just didn't think it would go this far. I'm not a politician, I'm just a guy. But the people voted for me, and I think it's actually a good thing that I'm not a politician and just a guy. I think might be the best guy to represent the people of South Carolina in the United States Senate."

It would have been a refreshingly honest moment, but he didn't say that. He didn't say anything. The story ends there because Mr. Greene lost his bid for the U.S. Senate seat in South Carolina.

I have something of a reputation for asking questions other anchors can't, or won't, ask. When I interviewed C. Ray Nagin, the former mayor of New Orleans for the fifth anniversary of Katrina, I took along a Ray Nagin coloring book. I found it at a little independent bookstore that was chocked full of goodies about New Orleans politics, community organization and government. The coloring book was beyond irreverent. It actually included an image of the former mayor in bunny ears, stirring a big old pot of chocolate.

The reference was clear: in the aftermath of Katrina when much of the black population had been bussed away from the city and it seemed like no efforts were made to provide any housing or rebuilding for those poor blacks whose homes had been destroyed, then-Mayor Nagin announced stridently that black New Orleans would return.

"This city was a chocolate city before Katrina, and it will be a chocolate city at the end of the day," he declared.

The backlash began almost immediately.

I wanted to ask him about that comment and what he thought about it five years later. I decided the coloring book would be the perfect way to introduce the topic.

"Have you seen this?" I asked handing him the book. His brow furrowed. It was pretty clear that he didn't find the coloring book's content the slightest bit humorous. "Looks like someone had a good time with the 'chocolate city' remark," I continued. "You remember that, right?"

"Remember it?" Nagin said darkly. "Like I'm ever going to forget."

He went on to talk about the true sentiment that he'd been trying to express and how the words he'd spoken had done more harm than good. It was a good interview and the coloring book ended up being the perfect way to introduce an uncomfortable topic. Instead of becoming defensive, Mr. Nagin was more relaxed and reflective, and I felt, gave a more genuine answer.

There have been times, however, when I've asked very pointed questions and expressed far less concern over the subtleties. A good example occurred during Glenn Beck's rally to "Restore Honor" held on August 28, 2010 at the Lincoln Memorial. You'll recall there was a lot of discussion surrounding this event because it was planned for the same date and place as Dr. Martin Luther King's "I Have a Dream" speech 47 years before.

Now before you put me in the black box and require me to condemn Glenn Beck, his message, his network, his rally and everything else, let me tell you that I think Glenn Beck has to right to do whatever he wants to do as long as it's not infringing on anyone else's protected liberties. If he wants to "reclaim the Civil Rights movement" he has the right to try it. I'm not really a fan, but then again, I've seen maybe five minutes of his show, not enough to really make an informed judgment about it. But I'm also pretty sure my show doesn't appeal to him either, so we'll just score that one even. My point is that Mr. Beck is within his rights. I don't know that I believe he's sincere, but I believe he has the right to rally, the right to march, and the right to say what he wants to say.

But I also think that when conservatives choose to congregate at the foot of the Lincoln Memorial on the anniversary of a moment in black history as significant as Dr. King's "I Have A Dream" speech, they are raising the same kinds of questions about insensitivity that the issue of a mosque near Ground Zero raises. It's not that it's wrong for Muslims to build mosques or for Conservatives to adopt civil rights, but there are definitely matters of feeling, and a sense of appropriateness, even of sacredness that must be addressed. Conservatives can't claim ignorance of those sensitivities in one circumstance, then lay claim to them in the next. Instead, they have to understand and respect what the Civil Rights movement means to so many Americans.

I'm not really discussing religion here. Religious freedom was a basic tenet of the founding of this country, it's one of the reasons the English left England to settle here. I have nothing against anyone's church, though I have found it to be oppressive when some assume that in order to be moral, right and correct, you must belong to a certain faith and follow its rules. The independent part of me resists that. Do I want to join a certain group, or am I an individual that makes decisions on my own, relying on my own faith?

I personally choose the latter.

I was taught moral principles in Catholic school and in my family's church. But everyone's an individual. Not everyone is suited for the same point of view. Not everyone can believe in the same way. I think people should investigate their beliefs. To the Buddhist, I say "Namaste." To the Muslim, "As-salamu alaykum." To the Jew, "Shalom." But choosing one faith over another doesn't confer upon anyone the right to pass judgment on others who don't act or worship or believe as you do.

For me, religion or God or whatever is all encompassing. I don't live my life with the concrete knowledge that everything in the Bible is what will happen or has happened or is completely true. But I live my life as if it's true, that being right and good, that attempting to live like Jesus is the right thing. The words "as if" are a subtle yet important distinction, especially for believers prone to extremism. My understanding is that all that is required is the faith of the mustard seed, which is pretty small. Just a little faith. I don't think the Bible requires us to believe fully and completely. No, just a little bit of faith. A mustard seed.

Whatever your religion, though, if your idea is to wipe someone out, I'm betting you're going against God every time. If that's the way it is, if we're all going to wipe out everyone who doesn't believe the same exact things we do, well, that's it for us. We're talking about the end of the world because we're not *ever* going to all believe the exact same thing. In the introduction I wrote that at first I felt like writing a book was narcissistic, and maybe it is. But the height of narcissism is to try to terminate others because they aren't exactly like you.

But I digress. I was talking about interviewing, and asking tough, pointed questions.

As you may recall, Al Sharpton also held a rally on August 28, 2010 to honor Dr. King and to protest Beck's gathering. The two men traded barbs in speeches in their competing rallies. CNN had reporters and producers covering both events, and I was in the studio in Atlanta asking them questions about what they had heard and seen.

A producer covering the Beck rally told us that Beck had asserted that if his rally wasn't diverse, neither was Sharpton's.

"Is that true?" I asked immediately. "You're there, looking at the crowds. What do you see?"

The producer hesitated and then babbled a non-answer. I was undeterred, but still didn't get a sufficient answer. Unfortunately, my time was up and I had to let it go.

During the break, I heard later, the cell phones in the newsroom began buzzing with a note from the head of our political unit. "Don Lemon just asked 'the' question, the one everyone wants the answer to. Make sure we get an answer to that question!"

To me, the question seemed completely obvious. We're talking about Civil Rights. We're talking about what we've been told is a predominantly white, conservative movement taking up the mantle for a new civil rights movement. We're talking about what we've been told is a predominantly black counter-demonstration. I'm just asking for verification. Was this white versus black, or was there diversity?

I'm not sure why this is so sensitive and makes so many journalists uncomfortable. Would saying, "Beck's crowd appears to be mostly white; Sharpton's mostly black" be racist, if it was a simply a statement of fact?

I don't see how, but the hesitation in the producer's response makes me wonder. It's a pretty sad comment on race relations if we can't even acknowledge that some people are black and some are white. Unfortunately, it's something I notice all too frequently in my business. In many stories, race gets talked "around" instead of approached head-on.

To my mind, that's infinitely more dangerous.

Whether it's confrontational or sympathetic, the art of interviewing anyone, whether it's an average person, a famous one,
or even a fellow reporter, is in the *listening*. Listening is the key.
You have to be paying attention to what's said and not on asking
your prepared questions. You have to be ready to get your head
out of your notes and pull out a coloring book, if that's what it
takes!

I've seen too many interviews where the interviewer is so worried about asking the next question that he or she is just *not
listening* to the answers. The result?

Missed opportunities.

I'm not sure you can really learn to interview. I think much
of it is innate, or comes with learning to be confident enough to
shut up and let the silence fall between you and the subject. Most
people don't like silence, especially on TV, but that's why it's so
useful. When the silence gets to the interviewee, they'll feel the
need to fill it and they'll start talking. They may say something
amazing, something shocking, and something unexpected.

When they do, it's going to create something memorable.

CHAPTER 18

A Lesson in
Embracing Change

Atruth we should all try to keep in the forefront of our
minds is simply this: Things are always changing.
Change is the one constant in our lives, in *all* aspects of our
lives.

Journalism is changing too, as technology makes it easier
for the average person to both create content and comment on
what's happening in the world. New technologies mean new
shifts in the way news is reported and collected, and by whom.

Personally, I think it's great: the technology, the connections, the fresh voices, the opportunities, all of it. I'm excited by what the future of journalism might be.

Follow me on Twitter (donlemoncnn) and you'll see my love of social networking first hand.

I tweet before I go on the air. I tweet during breaks. I ask viewers for their thoughts, their questions, and their feedback. I respond to the replies they post. I believe in social media and what it contributes to making sure that people like me remain relevant to the viewers in this fast-paced world.

I've always embraced technology, both for my job and in my life. My idea of happiness is browsing the tech stores and I've got just about every new gadget that comes out. I love the immediacy of it. I love the innovation of it. And I love all the things it allows us to do. Every since I started vlogging from Africa, I've recognized the impact of immediate feedback from the viewing audience can have on journalism. The Internet and social media have changed every aspect of our lives—including the way news is reported, collected, verified and assessed.

It's also news itself.

Take Craigslist.com for example. It's a networked yard sale in some ways, but it also puts people together in every other kind of way, for good or ill. I know you've read or seen some of the horror stories that have resulted from some Craigslist connections, including murders, rapes, and swindles of various kinds, but in 2006, when I did my first story on it, the site was just beginning to emerge as a mainstream alternative means of locating goods and services.

The concept was simple: I decided I wanted to find out if one could live an entire day on Craigslist, getting everything one needed from connections made on the site. We treated it like a reality TV show. We set up a camera and I locked myself in my apartment. Then I started thinking about what I'd like to with my day on Craigslist.

I decided to take a voice lesson. I made contact with an instructor and I said, "I want a lesson. Can you do it today?"

"Sure," the instructor said and came over a few hours later. I had a voice lesson.

I decided I wanted a mural, a map of the world, painted over my bed. I found an artist.

"Can you do it today?"

He came over and did it. It was fabulous—good enough that it was featured in a home magazine a few months after the story aired.

Food, of course, was easy to get and have delivered. I ate off Craigslist.com all day. The trickiest thing was I decided I wanted a dog. Pets are easy enough to find on the site, but my problem was my homeowner's association didn't allow pets in the condo I lived in. So I requested a "part-time" dog, available for me to pet and play with, but it couldn't stay. You guessed it: found on Craigslist.

Of course, I interviewed Craigslist founder, Craig Newmark. Like a lot of Internet innovators, I found him approachable and enthusiastic. He was really happy to talk about the site and about how it, and other social media, would eventually change the world.

In the few short years since I did that piece, it's obvious that he's quite right. Increasingly, the Internet brings everything we want right to our door and connects people in ways that we never expected. It's also had a tremendous impact on journalism.

There are some who argue that, at this point, the technology has evolved to the point that traditional journalism is nearly obsolete. Many people, even in the Third World, have cell phones and many of those phones have cameras. Which means cameras are everywhere and people can and do use them to capture events of monumental significance in ways that call into question the necessity for a full-scale "news organization" with its editorial hierarchy and its cumbersome bureaucracy. Instead, these "citizen journalists" are capturing history as it is being made, and in its unadulterated form, in ways that were absolutely unheard of before.

One of the best examples of this phenomenon was the Iranian elections in 2009 and the mass protests that followed the re-election of Mahmoud Ahmadinejad. There was a lock-down on journalists within the country, both Iranian and foreign. Traditional media was unable to get the message out of the country, and so we turned to social media, to Twitter and to Facebook, among others, to help us find out what the situation was in the country. Information that wasn't permitted out of the country through traditional media was spread quickly on Facebook and Twitter, enabling the world to catch a glimpse of what was happening in an extremely repressive society. Meanwhile, the protesting crowds kept swelling as more and more people responded to what many felt to have been a rigged vote. How did these outraged Iranians learn about the masses of people gathering in protest?

Social media.

When someone captured the shooting of Neda Agha-Soltan, a 22 year old student, on a camera phone, the story and the images went around the world. That's the power, and the immediacy of citizen journalism, and I respect it tremendously.

That story seems to suggest that citizen journalism can replace traditional journalism, especially in repressive regimes like Iran, but there's a lot more to it than that. While Iranians were twittering and Facebooking, CNN had reporters all over the region in various bureaus who were working with their sources, verifying the accuracy of what was being posted on social media. There were "big media" journalists working in Iran who were checking to make sure that the video being posted on the social media sites had occurred in real time and wasn't something shot a year ago, or created just for the web by a kid with pretensions of becoming the next Martin Scorsese. Creating a fake video is easy enough to do, after all.

The point is, in situations like the aftermath of the Iranian election, there are limits to social media. There are problems in its veracity and its accuracy and those problems illustrate why traditional media is still very much needed in spite of the prevalence and power of citizen journalism or "backpack journalism."

Social media by its nature is individual reporting, subject to all the limitations of individual perception at best and to unadulterated manipulation at worst.

Let's just be honest. Those pictures were broadcast on television all over the world because they were shown not on Facebook, but on a platform as large and as well-respected CNN. Social media made us aware of many of the atrocities, but traditional media exposed them to the masses. Traditional media broadcasted the video in the places where people congregate—in front of their television sets. Social media gave us access, but traditional news organization put the story out there for the world to see.

And there other truths, too. Like:

It helps to have an editor.
It helps to have training.
It helps to have a vetting process or fact-checkers.

These are the things that the citizen journalist doesn't have, and they are weaknesses. Individual journalism often lacks credibility because it's hard to tell what's fact, what's conjecture, what's opinion. That's the bedrock stuff of traditional journalism. Those are the first lessons you learn—verify your sources. Verify, verify, verify.

While I have my criticisms of it, I've embraced technology like social media. In fact, I've tried to use new technologies as much as possible for most of my career. When I vlogged from Africa, I wasn't there with the support of a news organization and a great deal of that trip aired solely on the Internet, accompanied by daily updates on my blog. I haven't stopped asking viewers to Tweet or Facebook when they want to add questions for a specific guest or respond to a story. I'm the guy who tested out Craigslist.com, remember? I completely understand that all of this innovation is going to change the news business—but I don't believe it will supersede it.

I was asked to talk about these ideas at the BlogWorld Conference in 2009 as a member of a panel entitled "The Death and Rebirth of Journalism" and it was a fairly spirited debate. Some of the panel, and some members of the audience, believed that traditional journalism had become too slow, too cumbersome, too political and too bureaucratic to respond appropriately to the fast-pace of the modern world.

I disagree.

I know that this is a time of transformation for traditional media. I know that we will eventually evolve in order to catch up to the immediacy of social media. But I truly believe that the two can co-exist. Not only co-exist, but thrive together.

A couple of the comments I made during that panel at BlogWorld 2009 got me into a bit of hot water with some people, however. While talking about the differences between citizen journalism and traditional media, I said that an advantage of "big media" is the sheer number of people available to check, double-check and triple-check the facts of a story. I was challenged on this point, because it suggested that only large media outlets like CNN, for example, care about the accuracy of their content.

That wasn't my intention. I do believe that all serious journalists, regardless of their resources, care that their reports are balanced and accurate. It's true that the more eyes and ears, the more sources, the more checks there are on the story the greater likelihood that mistakes and errors, if there are any, will be caught. Furthermore, those resources make it easier to uncover differing points of view and offer them up for fairness and balance. While I don't mean to suggest that backpack journalists are inaccurate, I do think the resources of big media contribute greatly to ensuring a higher degree of verification.

Then I started talking about the "size of my platform."

Oh, brother.

It started innocently enough as an exchange between me and a blogger in the audience.

"Big media is too big, too slow and too impersonal to be responsive to a fast-paced world," the guy asserted. "Because I'm independent, I can access sources that a news organization like CNN could never reach."

"You're right. There probably are places that an organization like CNN is too big to reach," I replied. But I also pointed out that the differences in size offered two approaches, each with something of value. Combined they offer something of unique added value to the consumer.

"The citizen journalist and big media need each other," I concluded. Working together, at least to me, seems to be in everyone's best interest, especially the viewer. Collaboration, to my mind, benefits the individual journalist by allowing his content to reach a larger audience.

"Working together makes sense," I concluded, "because, quite frankly, my platform is bigger than your platform."

Oooohh.

I think someone in the audience actually let out that word in a rush of breath. As I play it back now, it sounds a little like a hyper-masculine, schoolyard challenge: "My platform is bigger than your platform."

The audience member clearly took it that way, since he quipped back, "I decline that transaction."

It's funny when you look at it in hindsight, but in the moment, I'm afraid I might have sounded a little arrogant, even though it wasn't my intention.

The point I was trying make is simply that CNN is an international news organization. It *is* a big platform. It provides information to millions of people around the globe daily. Right now, at least, very few independent online news sites have the same reach. When we're able to partner with smaller, independent journalists and news organizations it's usually been a win-win-win—a win for CNN, a win for the independent journalist and a win for the viewer.

The way I said it was taken for "TV people" arrogance. Like I believed that because I'm on TV, I was somehow better than the independent guy. I wasn't thinking of myself like that, but I understand the perception my words might have created. It's something that I always have to guard against. I'm not an arrogant jerk and I really don't want to sound like one.

That exchange with the audience member at Blog World in 2009 was a little testy in spots, but it doesn't dim my enthusiasm for social media in the least. The truth still is that social media has upped my game. It's enabled me to get immediate feedback from my audience. Used to be, if there was an error in a story, you had to write a letter to the newspaper and then wait, or call the radio or TV station and then wait. Now, viewers and readers can use the Internet to respond to information immediately. Every day I get tweets, comments, and emails "Don, you got it wrong. The truth is x." Or "Why didn't you take that interview in this direction?" or "You missed something when you didn't explore that." Not every comment or tweet or correction is valid, but sometimes they are. They force me to be more careful, more thorough. Since I know I'll get feedback from the audience immediately, I try to be even more certain that what I'm reporting is verifiable and accurate. It forces me, and other journalists, to be more accountable.

Of course, I make mistakes. I'm human, but my job is to try to keep those mistakes down to a minimum and to check and check and check to make sure what I'm reporting is accurate. In this way, I see social media as a tremendous benefit to traditional media, in providing that immediate opportunity for comment and counterpoint.

I feel so strongly about this that I teach it when I can in an online course occasionally offered at Brooklyn College's School of Journalism. It's basically a class in "backpack journalism"—how to tell a story competently using all of the elements of the latest technology, but with all of the verification and reporting techniques of traditional journalism.

I'm teaching the next generation of journalists. These are the people who will ultimately fight the next battles between traditional journalism and its more individual, independent forms. Whether they follow a traditional path and sign on as a reporter in a small-market city, or load their cameras in their backpacks and head off on their own, they all need the bedrock skills of solid writing, checking and verifying sources, getting corroboration before using any material. I love that I have the opportunity to teach at Brooklyn College, the school that taught me, nurtured me, and believed in me. It makes the experience even more special.

Teaching makes me think about what I might do with the next phase of my life, after whatever comes after CNN, when I finally have that family that I think about sometime or when it's time to retire and take things slower.

Only recently did I make a real revelation about what I want to do and where I want to be when my career is over.

The answer surprised even me.

CONCLUSION: FULL CIRCLE

CHAPTER 19

A Lesson on the Word "Never"

They say "never say never" and it's a lesson I have personally learned.

In 1990, when I left Baton Rouge, I swore that I couldn't live
in the Louisiana anymore and I vowed never to do so again. I
struck out for New York, and only returned to visit family or
to volunteer in New Orleans for a week or two, but I couldn't
imagine myself ever being truly comfortable enough to live in
the state. For me, Louisiana had been the home of everything I
was trying to escape from—childhood torment, the loss of so

many people I loved, racism and limits on my ambitions and the constant feeling of being between worlds.

When I returned there with CNN to do the Katrina fifth anniversary report, something happened. Something changed.

I have always loved New Orleans. It is, and always has been, unlike any other city in America.

The city is slowly rebuilding and there was fresh energy in the air. The process is far from complete, of course, but I found myself mesmerized and engaged by the city in a way I hadn't been before. For the first time, in my many visits there since the hurricane's devastation, it *felt* like the New Orleans I remembered. Actually it felt better, since possibilities gleam from every corner. It's a city that survived near annihilation and, in the aftermath, has been gifted with the chance to re-invent itself as a real Renaissance City. It has the unique opportunity to be something entirely different, and make changes that couldn't have been made in the past without billions of dollars it didn't have and decades of work that no one would have waited for.

It's a city on the brink and its energy spoke to me.

Atlanta's energy is very different. When I'm home, I rarely find myself moved to get out of the house and walk the city. It isn't that kind of place. You could argue it's the weather, but New Orleans is every bit as hot, perhaps even hotter. I don't know. Perhaps it's the layout. Atlanta is spread out and landlocked. It's a modern city.

New Orleans was, and always has been, different.

After the 5th anniversary special finished, I stayed an extra week, walking and biking through the neighborhoods, talking to the people, looking at the homes. A little voice inside me began to whisper:

Yes, yes, yes.

I relaxed.

Those two words were everything—*I relaxed.* Relaxing isn't something I do very often. It wasn't something I had known I needed or wanted in my life until I found myself pausing at a sidewalk art show, or stopping to groove along with a street corner band. In my daily life, my phone is always buzzing. It's always vibrating with messages about work with invitations and requests. Even when I'm at home, there's work I need to do: expenses I needed to file, my taxes, errands, and relationships that need tending. There's always something I need to be doing, but I'd really just like to just veg. It has always created a vicious cycle of frustration and guilt: frustration because I just want to rest, and Guilt because I feel like I shouldn't.

It is part of the reason I work so much. When I'm working, I'm single-minded. At home, I've often felt divided. What I have to do, and what I want to do are splitting me into two opposing selves.

This is not what I want.

I want to be *re-energized* by my home. I want a sense of place. I want to feel connected. I want to wake up in the morning with the absolute certainty that I am where I belong.

During this recent visit, New Orleans, a city that I have always loved, gave me that. I had finished my work and New Orleans was giving me permission to play. I thought New Orleans had changed, but after a conversation with a brother in a little hole in the wall bar, I realized that although the city was making progress, the transformation would take more than simply money and re-built homes.

For New Orleans to change, *attitudes* have to change. No more *laissez faire,* no more *bon temps rouler.* No more "serve me" or "you owe me." Self-help is what will create this new New Orleans.

I have told you—I'm far more conservative than the black box character that some try to foist on all black journalists.

I ended up in this conversation with a guy in a bar while waiting to meet some friends. We covered the gamut. We talked about what it's like working for CNN, we talked about his work in the kitchen of a local restaurant. But mostly, we talked about New Orleans. Everything he said about why the recovery hadn't reached him was an excuse.

"You don't know the Seventh Ward," he kept saying. "You don't know the Ninth Ward."

"No, I don't," I agreed. "I don't know where you're from. I don't know New Orleans like you do . . . but I'm telling you. It's all what you make it, man. No one owes you anything. If you hang around waiting for what you think is owed you, you'll never have anything. You have to do it yourself."

"But you don't know this city. You don't know how things work here—"

"No, I'm not from New Orleans. I'm from Baton Rouge, an hour and half up the road," I replied. "And let me tell you, I have lived with discrimination, I have lived with racism, and I have lived around poor people. This attitude you're spouting, this "ain't nothing I can do, it's the system" is part of the problem. If you believe that New Orleans is intractable, that things will never be better, then you're part of the problem. It's defeatist."

The man stared at me. I realized that it was kind of odd that we were having this debate. He was big guy, easily two of me, and this was his home turf, not mine. He had that "tough guy" way of holding himself that many men who have been to prison have. He might have been to prison. Our conversation didn't include that revelation. As he measured me in silence, I wondered if I'd made a mistake by speaking so candidly.

"You got a smart mouth, but you make a lot of sense," he said at last.

Perhaps, at last, through time on the planet, I've gained some wisdom. Or maybe it's simply that, having lived long enough on this planet, I've finally learned to shut up and listen. Or maybe I've finally gotten to know myself enough. I've been alone enough, done enough things that scared and challenged me to be able meet new people, all kinds of people, and hear what they're saying without trying to change them. Maybe, though, you can put an idea in their heads that wasn't there before.

Maybe, it's only when you believe in yourself that you can believe in someone else.

I met musician Irvin Mayfield, who has a jazz playhouse in the hotel where we stayed. He was the one who brought jazz back to Bourbon Street after Katrina and he did it by working a deal with the Royal Sonesta to have music there every evening. He wanted to not only bring the musicians back but to improve the situation a bit by giving them a venue other than street corners to play.

He did it, not with a handout, but with will and heart and hard work.

He took me to a hole in the wall jazz club in the Seventh Ward called "Bullets." The great Kermit Ruffins was playing, a Grammy award winning musician playing at this juke joint hole in the wall in the heart of the Treme neighborhood, where jazz lovers of all ages, of all backgrounds were crammed inside to listen, to sing and dance and eat barbeque from the truck outside.

Only in New Orleans.

It's still the most hospitable place ever, but crime in the city is rampant. For many in New Orleans, the mentality is not to work to rebuild, but to sell drugs and shoot people. The economy has suffered from years of neglect and reliance on oil and tourism, as well as years of thinking that everything is owed to you. It's a result of the Huey P. Long chicken in every pot form of government.

Yet, I stayed another day.

I went to see my friends Ken and Joe, guys who went to LSU with me. They left Baton Rouge, and moved to New Orleans years ago and when they heard I was in town, invited me to dinner.

Over drinks, I confided my new revelations to them.

"I feel at home here. I feel more at home here, than anywhere else on this earth."

"Well, duh," they said, almost simultaneously.

"I'm even thinking about buying a house."

They looked at each other.

"Finish your drink. We're going house hunting."

I didn't buy on that trip, but I did on the next. I'm now the proud owner of a vacant lot in the Marigny neighborhood in New Orleans. Soon, I'll meet with an architect. I have my own possibilities to consider.

New Orleans is where I will retire. I'm buying now for my future and thinking of my future in ways I never have before. Ways beyond the next assignment or the next position. I'm thinking about where I want to be when the studio lights go down and I'm too old and slow for the fast-paced world of news. Of course, Ken and Joe were right; it had to be New Orleans.

Duh.

Where else would I go?

I'm eager to participate in its renewal and to help it become the city I know it can be.

Now is the time.

For the first time I understood that it wasn't the South, it wasn't Louisiana that had limited me. After all, my life experiences have now taught me there's a bigot in every neighborhood. Sometimes you fight them with your fists, but mostly you fight them with your grace, your intelligence and your wit. You fight them by acknowledging them to be the scared little children they are.

I knew how to fight what I had feared. With that knowledge, the uneasiness was gone. I fell in love with Louisiana again. For the first time, I was able to embrace all the gifts the state has given me since I left it twenty years ago: open-mindedness, a sense of racial identity, an awareness of the ambiguity of life. Even the worst things that have happened to me turned out to have hidden gems that have helped to propel me on my way.

I stopped saying "no" to Louisiana, and for the first time in a very long time, I felt at home.

It's a powerful lesson. Perhaps one of the most powerful of all.

NOTES

NOTES

NOTES

NOTES